:30

SECONDS

To Common Sense

D1484517

"Common sense in 30 seconds? I'm Janet Folger. Join me for Reclaiming America!"

:30

SECONDS
To Common Sense

*Breaking Through the Clutter of
Cultural Confusion with God's Simple
Truth*

Janet L. Folger

Coral Ridge Ministries
Fort Lauderdale

The award winning Commentary team from left to right: Chris Gorbey, Rich DeFilippo, Janet Folger, Greg Hoadley, and Jim Carter proudly display Excellence in Media's Angel Award and the National Religious Broadcaster's Genesis Award.

Here's how the work gets done: from left to right, Rich DeFilippo, Chris Gorbey, me, Barry Kase, Greg Hoadley, and Jim Carter.

This book is dedicated to the faithful who've been on the frontlines and in the trenches of the cultural war for decades waiting for the rest of us.

To you I say, help is on the way.

*We have stood firm. We have fought hard.
Now it's time to take the land.*

:30 Seconds To Common Sense: Breaking Through the
Clutter of Cultural Confusion with God's Simple Truth

Cover photo by Kelly Rusin.

The CENTER FOR RECLAIMING AMERICA is an outreach of
Coral Ridge Ministries to inform the American public and
motivate Christians to defend and implement the biblical
principles on which our country was founded.

Phone: (877) SALT-USA (725-8872); Fax: (954) 351-3325;
E-mail: cfra@crministries.org;
Web: www.reclaimamerica.org

CORAL RIDGE MINISTRIES
P.O. Box 40
Fort Lauderdale, FL 33302

Printed in the United States of America

Table of Contents

Introduction

So you're sitting in the office, the salon, or in the university lounge after class. And those around you are talking about . . . pick a subject . . . any subject . . . let's say . . . evolution. "How could any-one believe in creation?" says one. "Pleeeease! You'd have to be an idiot to believe that!" exclaims another. "Everyone knows that it took millions and millions of years for us to evolve."

After all, they learned it in school.

What would you say?

Have you ever kept quiet because you didn't want to look stupid? You may believe that God created the earth and all, but you don't know anything that backs that up except that it says so in Genesis. The only problem is that this doesn't mean much to people who don't take the Bible literally.

You see, on issues I didn't know much about, I would just keep quiet. (Those who know me say that's hard to imagine.) So rather than do any damage to my position, lots of times I wouldn't speak up at all. After all, I didn't want to look stupid.

And now, the big fear drilled into people's minds is the unforgivable sin, to be called "intolerant." And all you need to receive the label of "intolerant" is to disagree with the "politically correct" establishment. Kind of reminds me of a bumper sticker I once had with the definition of a "Bigot: 1.(n) a conservative who is winning a debate with a liberal." That's not far off target. "Name-calling is a common response from those who can't back up their positions with logic and reasoning.

Like the issue of homosexuality. You had better never disagree with a homosexual activist, or "bigot" is just the beginning of what you will hear. If you have the audacity to actually voice anything other than the "party line," you will be accused of "hate speech," or called an "intolerant homophobe." Welcome to free speech in the 21st Century.

About five years ago I didn't know much about homosexuality—except that the Bible said it was an "abomination" somewhere. I hoped people wouldn't practice it for their own sakes, but as long as they didn't force it on the rest of us, I didn't much care. "Tolerance," and "Live and let live"—weren't these their mantras? I was fine with that until I learned that "live and let live" meant we would be forced to accept it, embrace it, celebrate it, subsidize it, teach it, and force it on every institution, organization, and citizen, regardless of what they really believed. If they resisted, this "tolerance" would demand that they be slandered, silenced, re-educated, re-located (from public property), fined, penalized, and criminalized. Welcome to the "tolerance" of the 21st Century.

I had absolutely no idea how much this issue alone affected me or the direction of this nation. I didn't have a clue that it threatened our freedoms of speech, association, and religion. You will see real-world examples on this subject and just what is at stake. If the Church is silenced, I'm convinced that this issue will be what does it—if we let it.

Then there's pornography; another subject to which I didn't pay much attention. It wasn't really discussed much in the Folger household. But a whole lot of people do pay attention to it. According to *U.S. News & World Report*, pornography went from a $10 million business in 1973 to a $10 billion dollar business in 1999. Now, according to *Forbes* magazine, it's up to $56 billion worldwide. That's more than the domestic receipts of all of our American movies, and more than rock-and-roll and country music profits *combined*.

But it's just "harmless entertainment" that doesn't really have any impact on society—right? Think about the amount of money spent on a sixty-second ad for the Super Bowl. Why do companies spend millions for just sixty-seconds? Well, it's not to entertain. It's to change the behavior of those watching . . . to get them to *do* something.

Now think about tens of billions being spent on pornography. And the hours, weeks and months spent watching it. Think that might influence behavior? When Oklahoma City closed its sexually orientated businesses, the rape rate dropped 25 percent, while the rest of the state's rape rates *rose* 20 percent. I think it does. If thoughts are not "taken captive," we will remain captives to our thoughts. And actions begin with thoughts. "For as he thinks in his heart, so is he" (Proverbs 23:7 NKJV).

Another chapter in this book deals with the assault against Christianity. I get pretty fired up about that and, well, that might have a bit to do with why there are so many commentaries on that subject. That, along with the fact that it's happening everywhere you turn.

Take what's happening in Canada, for example. Michael Horowitz, an American intellectual leader against the anti-Christian persecution, says the situation with Christians in Canada has many parallels with the Jewish experience. Evangelicals are the "new Jews of the 21st century," he recently told *Christianity Today*. "Every statement used to distance oneself from Jews is now being said about Christians. It's utterly striking how verbatim the same language is used in newsrooms, at fancy dinner parties, in faculty clubs." And we're not much better off than our neighbors to the north.

Take a look overseas and you'll see things far, far worse. Christians in Sudan are being sold as slaves. They are being jailed, tortured, and killed there as well as in China, Pakistan, India, Indonesia, and Iran, just to name a few—persecution that hasn't been seen since the Roman Empire.

Whether we'd like to admit it or not, Christians are being silenced. Here and now.

Some because they are not sure of their beliefs.

Some because they feel inadequate to defend their beliefs.

Some are silent from fear of ridicule.

Others are silent because they don't know their

rights. They have bought the lies designed to keep us quiet. Like the so-called "Constitutional Separation of Church and State." That this lie is so widely accepted today proves the axiom that if you say something loud enough and often enough, people actually believe it, even though it's not in our Constitution. And anyone could find that out by simply . . . reading it.

But that's too hard. Better to take the word of the courts, the liberal spokespeople and the media— sorry, I didn't mean to be redundant there. But that lie, perhaps more than any other, has sent Christians running for the hills.

Imagine the ACLU's perspective on the suggestion that we put the Bible in public schools! Think of their reaction to a statement like this:

"Should not the Bible regain the place it once held as a school book? Its morals are pure; its examples captivating and noble."

Who would suggest such a thing? No, not Dr. D. James Kennedy; and it wasn't Jerry Falwell. It was Fisher Ames, the guy who *wrote* the First Amendment. You see, he wrote about a disturbing trend in American education back in 1801: school teachers were making little use of the Bible.

(*Sound familiar?*) And Mr. Ames felt it necessary

to stand up and do something about it. Now here's another question that I have asked in my commentary: Who do you think best understands the meaning of the First Amendment—the guy who wrote it 200 years ago, or a bunch of ACLU lawyers today? You be the judge.

This book is chock-full of fun facts just like that. The purpose is to provide you with some not-so-common sense responses in an effort to take off the "gag" society has placed on those of us who might disagree with the prevailing propaganda.

Lutheran pastor Dr. Laurence White said it best: "We may be losing the cultural war, but we are losing by default!" We have not lost the ground in battle—we have willingly surrendered it. We have walked away from our influence in Hollywood, the media, our school boards, our city, county, state, and national legislative assemblies. We have retreated from battles where one voice, one objection, one lobbying effort would have changed the outcome. But there was no one willing to stand.

They had been chased off, scared off, or perhaps just too busy to know or care. They have been huddled behind the four walls of the church while our nation crumbles around us. And while some have been shoved into the closet, most of us have gone willingly. And while we sit, week after week, getting "strong in the Word," there never comes a point where we actually *use* that strength.

As Dutch Sheets illustrates in his book, *Intercessory Prayer*, we are like the body-builder showing off his bulging biceps to an African tribal chief. We know the Word. We're in church two and three times a week. But, as the African chief said to the muscle man, "What, exactly, do you *do* with all those muscles?" The body builder, anxious to demonstrate the results of his efforts, flexed his bulging muscles in several different poses, proudly awaiting affirmation. But the chief responded, "That's all you use them for?" The body builder replied, "Yes. That's pretty much it." And the chief responded, "What a waste. What a waste."

That is where we are in the Church. As my friend Ed Kasputis observed, when looking for Christians to help him go door to door in his run for the state legislature, he heard mostly, "No. I can't. I have Bible study." "Can't, choir practice." "Sorry, church night." All good things to do. But his response to me was, "We're in the Super Bowl, and they're still doing push-ups."

Let me ask you a question: Do you love God? Jesus said that if you love Him, you'll keep his commandments. In other words, you love Jesus when you *do* what He says. If you know the Word, you are expected to obey it, to use it to make a difference. To whom much is given, much is required

(Luke 12:48). And contrary to the separate societies in which we've found ourselves living, we are told to be salt and light in this decaying and dark world, to preserve and to shine—not ignore.

But we have been ignoring what's happening outside. While we've been doing push-ups, there's a game going on. Only it's more important than any Super Bowl. It's the battle for the future of this nation.

If you've spoken up, you know the hostility with which they wage their "tolerance." Do you want to know why they hate us? Because we, the Christians, are the *only* ones standing in the way of their getting everything they want.

This last presidential election should tell you just how close the battle lines are drawn. We are on the brink, and I don't think that after a "36-day election" I need to say how every vote and every voice counts.

Yet we have been in hiding so long that when we finally do venture out from behind the closet door, we're treated like trespassers. That's where we are now. Wait much longer to use your voice, and you're going to find a padlock on the outside of that closet door.

You see, if you don't use your First Amendment

rights, you will lose them. It's as simple as that. Use them or lose them. The choice is yours.

How? That's what this book is all about: Letting the truth of God's Word penetrate the prevailing thought, shining the light of His truth into the deep-rooted shadowy lies, and exposing the hypocrisy, as well as the devastation and destruction left in their wake.

Rather than sitting by while the "politically correct" slogans are being exchanged on the "subject du jour," you may have something to add, something to shake them up a bit. It's really kind of fun, once you've tried it. They're not used to anyone challenging them, and when someone does, well, let's just say you'll catch them off guard. But be sure to brace yourself for name-calling like you haven't experienced since the second grade. Disagree in the second grade and you're called a "meanie." Disagree with them now and well, you're "mean-spirited." And you just know they're going to run and tell the teacher. "Waaaaa." (You watch, I'll get letters for that!)

And while our culture may appear morally deaf, I believe sound bites—nuggets of truth—can penetrate beyond the prevailing propaganda. God's Word won't return void after all. The truth *will* prevail. But for it to prevail, it must be spoken. Speaking that truth may mean that when the "enlightened" establishment speaks of the fabric of their "elite" society—pointing out the style and sophistication of their material, the satin-like shine and glimmer of their positions—that we stand up and shout, "The emperor has no clothes!"

While common sense may not be all that common, maybe, just maybe, if we all found the courage to enter into the discussion in the office, the salon, or the lounge after class, the common sense of God's perspective could be voiced, heard, and yes, even acted upon, to change the course of discussion, direction, and even this nation.

It all begins with you.

This is what the final TV version looked like to the viewers.

This is what the viewers *didn't* see. Greg and I brainstorming: "I don't know, what do *you* want to write about?"

Section 1

Abortion

Life: the issue that has dominated mine. For more than 20 years I have been in the pro-life battle—the human rights issue of our time. No other issue has had this many casualties. No disease. No war—not all of our wars *combined*. We've killed more than the population of Canada—more than 40 million in our nation alone.

And yet, the Church has been intimidated into silence on this issue. They'll say whatever works to keep us quiet: we can't talk about abortion in church—because it's a "*political issue.*" We can't talk about abortion in politics—because it's a "*religious issue.*" And against that stellar logic—Christians retreat.

Hey, I know a good book on the subject called *True to Life*; you just might want to stop by your local bookstore and order a copy. OK, OK, I *wrote* the book. But I still highly recommend it.

Proverbs 31:8 says, "Open your mouth for the speechless, in the cause of all who are appointed to die" (NKJV), and yet how many Christians read this without obeying it?

Self-identified "born-again" Christians actually voted for the man who could have prevented partial-birth abortions from being done in this country. Yeah, President Clinton's the one who vetoed the bill to ban this act of killing children during delivery and yet Christians voted for him.

Why? Their pocketbook. As Dr. Kennedy has said, "I hope they're happy with their pocketbook, because it has come at the expense of over 10 million lives" (in the last eight years alone).

Christians could stop abortion right now if they would simply NEVER vote for anyone in any election who supported any abortion. It would be over if we would just stand and obey God rather than the perception of a better pocketbook.

Yeah, I know what you're thinking: how do I *really* feel about this issue? These commentaries will give you a pretty good idea. They will highlight the outrageous disparity between what American law says is admissible and what our God-given insight and human instinct tells us is an affront to humanity—making this issue the human rights issue of our time.

It is my very strong belief (you'll find that a lot of my beliefs are that way) that one day we will win this battle. Aside from the fact that God is on our side—rather we are on God's side, we have the necessary ingredients for success: the truth, persistence, and love. We just need to rise up, join together, and act on every single one of them.

Stacey Mossop providing some finishing touches while Matt Johnston focuses.

Two-Year-Old

FOR YEARS WE'VE BEEN hearing that abortion is a "complicated" issue.

While speaking at the Ohio Statehouse, I found a two-year-old volunteer from the audience to settle this complex debate once and for all.

I held up a cover of *LIFE* magazine with a picture of the unborn entity on the front and asked, "What is this a picture of?" The two-year-old responded, "Baby."

I find it amazing that a two-year-old could recognize what half the elected officials could not. Of course, I was accused of prepping her with what to say . . . yeah! Until I told her it was a baby, I'm sure she was referring to it as a "product of conception." Right!

The pro-life movement has the truth that even a child can recognize. That's why pro-abortionists try so hard to hide it. It's really not so complicated.

Source: *Ohio State Lantern*, April 26, 1993

❧❧

The Bamboo Tree

IN THE FAR EAST people plant a tree called the Chinese bamboo. During the first four years they water and fertilize the plant with seemingly little or no results. But the fifth year they again water and fertilize—and in five weeks time the tree grows ninety feet in height!

Question: Did the Bamboo tree grow ninety feet in five weeks or five years? Answer: It grew ninety feet in five years, because if at any time the people had stopped watering and fertilizing the tree, it would have died.

Many times it seems as though our efforts have little or no results. For 25 years, abortion on demand has been legal. But if we are faithful to water and fertilize, and work and pray, we, too, will see results.

Nothing to Forgive

REMEMBER MELISSA DREXLER?

She's the mother who murdered her own baby after she delivered it in the bathroom during her high school prom. She wrapped the infant in several plastic bags and threw it in the garbage can.

In court she read a statement which included, "The baby was born alive. I was aware of what I was doing at the time when I placed the baby in the bag."

A reporter asked her father, John Drexler, whether he had forgiven his daughter. His reply? "There's nothing to forgive."

The chill of that statement is numbing. But in a society whose laws place no value on the life of a child prior to birth, why should this surprise anyone?

Source: *Asbury Park Press*, August 21, 1998

Mother Killed by Abortion

A POPULAR PRO-LIFE SLOGAN is that only half of the people who enter an abortion clinic come out alive. That's not exactly what happened in a Brooklyn clinic recently.

Twenty-two-year-old Tamika Dowdy was pronounced dead shortly after having obtained an abortion. She had been living with her boyfriend, rapper Rudy Alston. The two were planning on getting married but didn't want to have kids just yet.

After Alston found out his girlfriend was dead, he said, "I want that place closed down. I want that doctor arrested for murder."

He's right to call it murder, but I have a question: Which murder is he talking about—his girlfriend or his unborn child?

Rudy Alston deserves our condolences for both his losses—his girlfriend . . . and his child.

Source: *New York Post*, December 6, 1998

❧❦

The Coat Hanger Myth

IT'S BEEN SAID THAT if you repeat a lie often enough, it becomes the truth. In their new ad campaign, the National Abortion and Reproductive Rights Action League (NARAL) and other groups are saying that prior to *Roe v. Wade* many women died in back alleys just to get an abortion.

But guess what? They're lying. But don't take my word for it. Bernard Nathanson, who founded NARAL, now admits that he lied when he said that thousands of women died of illegal abortions.

Who else says the back-alley coat hanger abortions were a myth? The Centers for Disease Control and the American Journal of Obstetrics and Gynecology.

So the medical authorities and NARAL's founder call it a lie. Why does NARAL still repeat it?

Source: *New York Magazine*, November 23, 1998

Pro-Abortion Ads

COMING SOON TO A small screen near you, pro-abortion groups will soon be touting their empty rhetoric and soon-to-be released paid TV advertisements.

One ad features a young woman who says, "When I got pregnant, my best friend said I should have the baby. But I knew that abortion was the responsible choice for me."

Responsible? I guess that's just what Melissa Drexler thought when she threw her newborn baby away before going back to her high school prom.

Another woman who once had an abortion now says, "Someday you may be pregnant with a child that you want. Suddenly, the realization will dawn on you that, other than your own desires, there's no difference between the child you're carrying and the child you once carried." I bet you won't hear that in the pro-abortion ads.

Source: *Jewish World Review*, November 13, 1998

Right to Life of Insects & Fish

ON A RECENT EPISODE of a radio talk show, the host saw fit to slap one of his guests with a dead fish. Not exactly what I'd call entertainment.

A representative of People for the Ethical Treatment of Animals condemned this act because it "shows a disrespect for life, certainly for the lives of fish." Never mind the stupidity; we've got to respect those fish.

While shooting the hit film *Men In Black*, the producers were kept under the watchful eye of the American Humane Association to make sure they didn't mistreat the live cockroaches! We're looking at people with a little too much time on their hands.

You know society has lost its way when the rights of cockroaches and dead fish are considered greater than the rights of unborn babies.

Source: Columnist Brent Bozell, November 25, 1998

Romance in the 90's

IT STARTED OUT AS a typical romance for the '90s: Man meets woman, they fall in love, move in together, and talk about getting married someday. Maybe.

There was just one catch: Peter Wallis made his girlfriend, Kellie Smith, promise to stay on the pill and not get pregnant. But Kellie got pregnant, and she refused Peter's demands to get an abortion.

So Peter kicked her out of his apartment. That's not all he did! According to the *Washington Post*, he sued Kellie for becoming pregnant against his will and forcing him into fatherhood—a role he didn't choose.

So what does this mean? Peter has fallen prey to the 90's idea that the recreative and procreative roles of sex are separate. Like it or not, the two go together. Suing your girlfriend or killing your child won't change that.

Source: Columnist Brent Bozell, November 25, 1998

Matthew Shepard & the Death Penalty

LAST OCTOBER, HOMOSEXUAL MATTHEW Shepard was brutally murdered. The CENTER FOR RECLAIMING AMERICA immediately denounced this horrible crime. Many Christian groups have even called for the death penalty for his killers.

Just recently, a prominent organization opposed the death penalty in this case. What group, you ask? The ACLU.

That's right! In a recent press release, they opposed the death penalty because "the state should not have the power to take away human life." Excuse me?

This is from the group that opposes the death penalty, yet supports abortion?

Here's the difference: one's innocent and one's guilty. The ACLU is only interested in protecting the guilty.

Source: ACLU press release, January 21, 1999

❧❧

Women and Abortion

FAYE WATTLETON IS THE former Executive Director of Planned Parenthood. Just recently, she conducted a poll to find out what women really think about abortion. I am sure she hoped the poll would confirm her own views, but she was in for a surprise: Her results showed that the majority of women consider themselves pro-life.

Naturally, she was hoping for a different result. You know, maybe one that would have justified all that money Planned Parenthood has taken from vulnerable young women. Maybe that's why she called the poll results "very disturbing."

Don't expect to see these results advertised anywhere by Planned Parenthood. Another pro-abortion myth exposed to its worst enemy—the truth.

Source: Media Research Center press release, January 29, 1999

Ask the Professionals

IT IS COMMON IN today's society to hear opinions on abortion from a host of different groups. But what do the professionals think? You know: the doctors and nurses who are in the hospitals and clinics.

Well, since 1988, the number of doctors who would not work in an ob-gyn unit that performs abortions has risen from 48 to 61%.

Of nurses in the same field, the numbers who will not consent to work in the same unit has risen from 45 to 63%.

How many of us would participate in something that the majority of experts wouldn't even go near? If 61% of doctors wouldn't even go into the room where you were going to have surgery, would you?

Source: *CultureFacts*, March 24, 1999

Baby Named "Hope"

IS ABORTION JUST A lifestyle choice, as proponents claim? Well, listen to this.

A woman in Dayton, Ohio, had just begun a partial-birth abortion process, which takes three days. She was 5fi months pregnant, but that night she experienced abdominal pains and was rushed to the hospital. She gave birth to a little girl, whom the nurses named "Hope." The nurses desperately tried to save the premature baby. Some of them even took turns holding Hope and singing to her. But despite their efforts, she died.

According to a statement released by the hospital, the nurses are traumatized. Far from just another lifestyle choice, they say their pain "is deeper and will last longer than all their other (cases)."

Source: *Jewish World Review*, May 17, 1999

Abortion Without Consent

THINK PUBLIC SCHOOLS ARE a safe place for children? Think again.

Howard and Marie Carter did not want their daughter to have an abortion. Since she is a minor living in Pennsylvania, she had to have parental consent.

However, William Hickey, a guidance counselor at their daughter's school, arranged for an abortion to be performed across state lines in New Jersey— where parental consent is not required.

He also organized the financing and wrote notes to her teachers excusing her absences, and guess what? The school is backing the counselor, not the parent.

The Carters agreed to a public education for their daughter; what they got was betrayal and a dead grandchild.

Source: *Washington Watch*, August 23, 1999

☞☜

Choosing Something Wonderful?

A FULL COLOR, GLOSSY brochure invites abortionists to "find out how you can turn your patient's decision into something wonderful."

What's wonderful? Get baby body parts. Opening Lines, a wholesale trafficker in aborted baby parts, pays $75 for babies' eyes and ears, and up to $1000 for a brain.

Hey, aren't these the same people who say this is just a glob of tissue? And now they're bulk ordering eyes, ears, and baby's brains—ready to ship coast to coast.

And this is what they call "something wonderful?" "Woe to those who call evil good, and good evil" (Isaiah 5:20).

Source: *Life Site News*, August 22, 1999

Margaret Sanger & Minorities

JOHNNY HUNTER, A BLACK pastor, recently proclaimed on the steps of the U.S. Supreme Court, "Even though we make up 12% of the population, we supply 33% of the abortion industry's business." He added, "We have fallen prey to Margaret Sanger's plan for the black race." And what was that plan?

Sanger, the founder of Planned Parenthood, was motivated by her hatred of African Americans, and she specifically targeted them for abortion. She sought to promote it among the black community "through a religious appeal." In other words, Sanger wanted black preachers to do her work for her—all under the guise of family planning.

And as Reverend Hunter pointed out, her plan worked.

Source: *CultureFacts*, October 14, 1999

❦

Holding Hands

"SHH! YOU'LL WAKE THE baby!" That's what Dr. Bruner said as he began the surgery on Samuel Alexander Armas. Samuel is a 21-week-old unborn baby. As Dr. Bruner continued the surgery, a photographer clicked one of the most remarkable pictures ever taken. Little Samuel reached out from the womb during the surgery and clutched the doctor's healing hand.

At 21 weeks, Samuel could legally be aborted, but that was never an option for his parents. They chose the surgery because the baby's spina bifida could cause brain damage and they wanted the child to know them. Now Samuel, who is due on December 28, will get to know his parents and shake Dr. Bruner's hand again.

Source: *Drudge Report,* November 18, 1999

Carol Everett & the Truth of Sex-Ed

IS PLANNED PARENTHOOD DRUMMING up abortion business in your school?

Meet Carol Everett. She used to operate several abortion clinics. Today, she tells the truth about what she was really up to when she visited high schools. She says, "The first thing was to get the students to laugh at their parents. That way, they won't go home and tell their parents what I told them...[then] I'd say, 'Would your parents help you get . . . contraception if you become sexually active? Don't worry about that. Here's a card. Come to me.'"

She adds, "I knew that any time I went to a school, the pregnancy rate went up sharply . . . by my own statistics, and by working with Planned Parenthood and their statistics."

So why do it? More pregnancies mean more abortions.

Source: *New American*, November 22, 1999

❧☙

Abortion as Crime Prevention?

WE'VE BEEN HEARING PRO-ABORTION arguments for years. Well, now they've got a new one. Two professors from the Universities of Stanford and Chicago are saying that abortion prevents crime. They argue that the reason crime has gone down this decade is because many of today's criminals were actually aborted about twenty years ago.

So does that mean that a good anti-crime package should include killing innocent children before they're born, since they might grow up to do something wrong? Hey! Why not do the same for five-year-olds if they sneak a cookie or tell a fib?

Forget about innocent until proven guilty. Since they can't defend themselves, let's not only kill them, but let's make ourselves feel better by blaming them for murder as well.

Source: *Jewish World Review,* August 13, 1999

Abortion Rate Declines

THERE'S SOME GOOD NEWS on the pro-life front: the abortion rates continue to decline. According to the U.S. Centers for Disease Control, the rate of abortion in 1997 was at its lowest point since 1975.

The credit has to go to the pro-lifers, who have volunteered time at Right to Life groups and to thousands of pregnancy crisis centers across this country. These centers offer counseling, information and adoption referrals to young mothers, free of charge. Meanwhile, abortion clinics charge about $300 for each unborn child they kill.

Pro-lifers, your efforts saved over 1,300 babies a day compared to where we were ten years ago.

What you do matters!

Source: *CNN Online*, January 6, 2000

The Delhi Sands Fly

THE U.S. FISH AND Wildlife Service recently forced builders in California to stop construction of a $500 million development project. Why? Because eight Delhi sands flies were spotted near the sight. You see, the Delhi sands fly is on the Endangered Species list. So anyone found guilty of harming one could face a $25,000 fine and possible jail time.

Meanwhile, partial-birth abortion is still legal. That is where an abortionist plunges scissors into a baby's neck and then uses a machine to suck the child's brains out.

So according to our government, harming an insect is a terrible crime—but killing human babies through partial-birth abortion? Well, that's okay.

Source: *Savior's Seasonings,* Januray 2000

Abortion Regulations

IN VIRGINIA LAST MONTH a House committee voted 14 to 7 to defeat a bill that would require most abortion facilities to comply with hospital guidelines—something they currently don't do.

Pro-life Delegate Robert Marshall said, "If so-called access to safe health care is the goal of abortion supporters, they should embrace this proposal."

But a spokesman for Planned Parenthood Advocates of Virginia said, "This would effectively shut down every [abortion] clinic in the state."

Really! If implementing basic hospital guidelines would shut down every abortion facility, then they're in much worse shape than we thought.

Sounds like they need those guidelines pretty badly.

Source: *The Virginian-Pilot*, February 13, 2000

Planned Parenthood Profits

EVERY YEAR, PLANNED PARENTHOOD gets $176 million of our taxes. This might lead you to believe that they don't make enough money off of manipulating vulnerable young pregnant women to get abortions. But guess what? The numbers say otherwise.

Every year since 1995, their margin of profit has increased, even while their federal funding has not been cut. In fact, in their latest annual financial report, their records showed a $125 million profit margin.

Let's do the math. We give Planned Parenthood $176 million, and they get to keep a $125 million profit after expenses. What's wrong with this picture?

Source: *STOPP Press Release*, February 21, 2000

Ventura Vetoes Right-to-Know

PRIOR TO ALMOST ANY surgical procedure, doctors are required by law to give their patients all the facts about the operation . . . except for abortion.

That's why the Minnesota State Legislature recently passed a "Woman's Right-To-Know" bill. If it had become law, it would have guaranteed that women would be presented with all the facts—and possible consequences—prior to an abortion. Sounds pretty reasonable, right?

Well, Minnesota Governor Jesse Ventura didn't think so. He vetoed the bill, claiming to be pro-choice. But women need information to make an informed choice, don't they? He says he's pro-woman. Women can't be hurt by information.

No, Governor Ventura is pro-abortion, plain and simple.

Source: *Washington Post*, April 14, 2000

Abortion Clinic: Unlicensed

A RECENT OHIO DEPARTMENT of Health investigation revealed that the Dayton Women's Services and the Capitol Care Women's Center abortion clinics were not only unlicensed, but also unsanitary and unsafe. Supplies were outdated and there were no labels to identify some drugs. Unsterilized equipment was used, including rusty forceps, and the same gloves were used both to clean up and to prepare rooms for the next patient.

The Health Department report recommended their licenses not be approved. The director of the Capitol Care abortion clinic responded that other abortion clinics in Columbus are not licensed either. Thanks for the tip. The Ohio Health Department should visit them next.

Source: Ohio Department of Health, Investigation of Complaint, October 27, 1999

Abortion in Poland

PRO-ABORTION ADVOCATES HAVE been telling us for decades that if abortion were outlawed, it would result in illegal, back-alley abortions. But one country has proven them wrong. For over 40 years Poland was dominated by Russia, where abortion was not only legal, but paid for by the government.

But in 1993, after the Iron Curtain fell, the Polish parliament restricted abortions. By last year, the annual abortion rate had gone from over 160,000 to only 250. Not only that, fewer women died as a result of pregnancy and childbirth, and premature births declined after the pro-life laws were passed.

Hey, it worked in Poland. Why not try it here?

Source: *Family News In Focus*, May 10, 2000

NY Times **and Abortion**

Is there a constitutional amendment that allows abortion on demand?

According to the *New York Times*, there is. In a recent story, reporter Richard Berke referred to a "constitutional amendment allowing abortion."

But there's just one problem: there *is* no constitutional amendment allowing abortion. A constitutional amendment requires passage in both houses of Congress by a two-thirds majority, and passage in three-fourths of the states.

But abortion was legalized by the judicial tyranny of seven unelected judges on the Supreme Court, not the democratic process.

The *New York Times* may *wish* abortion was legalized by a constitutional amendment, but wishing it and *reporting* it doesn't make it true.

Source: *New York Times,* June 29, 2000

Ex-Abortionists: Why They Quit

Dr. Paul Jarrett began his career as a doctor in the early '70s by performing abortions. In 1974 he had a life-changing experience. While performing a routine abortion, the suction device became clogged by the baby's leg. He realized that this baby was too developed for a suction abortion, so he began to dismember the baby.

Jarrett describes the situation, " . . . as I brought out the rib cage, I looked and saw a tiny beating heart. And when I found the head of the baby, I looked squarely in the face of another human being—a human being that I just killed. . . . I knew I couldn't be a part of abortion anymore."

How many more dismembered babies will it take to convince the rest of them?

Source: *Human Life Review*, Summer 2000

RU-486 Marketed to Teens

The U.S. Food and Drug Administration just approved the abortion pill, RU-486. As if that wasn't bad enough, Planned Parenthood is marketing it to our teens.

Their website for kids gives them a hot-line number with no parental notification attached to it, telling them it's a "safe" procedure. Why is this a problem? Because with RU-486, you don't just pop a pill in your mouth and your pregnancy's over.

No. It's a three-step process that ends with the baby being aborted at home. You see, if the mother is seven weeks pregnant, she will be delivering her dead child, complete with arms, legs, fingers and toes.

And thanks to Planned Parenthood, this could happen to your teen, without your ever knowing about it.

Source: Family News In Focus, October 13, 2000

Pro-lifer's caged like cows

The Catholic Church, from the Pope, on down, has consistently taken a pro-life stand. So it should have been no surprise that pro-life Catholics protested when, Gonzaga (Catholic) University, hosted a rally featuring vice-president Gore. After all Mr. Gore made abortion on demand a cornerstone of his campaign. What was a surprise ... is how the vice-president's Secret Service contingent herded pro-life protestors into pens resembling livestock holding cells.

After being caged like an animal one protestor stated, "I was ... stunned that the viewpoint ... faithful to the Catholic faith ... was squelched with the collaboration of the (Catholic) university staff."

I agree! Does the Pope know about this?

Source: World Net Daily, October 27, 2000

☙❧

Is Abortion Because of Rape Okay?

If you look at the polls, you'll find that the majority of Americans are opposed to ninety-eight percent of all abortions. However, most people still support abortion on account of rape or incest.

But a new book called *Victims and Victors* documents nearly two hundred women who became pregnant by rape, and fifty-five children who were conceived as a result. And what do they have to say? Over ninety percent of these victims and their children say they would discourage other victims from getting an abortion, and every woman interviewed was glad she chose life.

One of the women, Kathleen DeZeeuw, concluded, "I feel personally assaulted…every time I hear that abortion should be legal because of rape and incest."

Source: Family News In Focus, November 1, 2000

One Couple's Abortion Struggle

What leads a woman to decide to take her unborn child's life?

Fred Minnick, an Oklahoma State University student, wrote a powerful article titled "One Couple's Struggle with Abortion." He told of how a young couple fell in love, and as a result of a bad decision, she became pregnant. Suddenly, they had a choice to make.

And yet, as the 18-year old girl lay on the abortionist's table, she and her boyfriend decided they couldn't go through with it. Minnick wrote, "The couple stormed out of the clinic." How did the story end?

Minnick concluded, "That couple… they were my parents, and eight months later, I was born…. A lot of people will say, 'you don't know until you're in that situation. I have been. Only I was inside."

Source: *Daily O'Collegian* (Oklahoma State University Newspaper), October 18, 2000

Peter Singer On Newborns

Princeton Bioethics Professor Peter Singer has said that "no fetus has the same claim to life as a person."

He explains why in his book, *Writings of an Ethical Life*, "these arguments [for killing unborn babies] apply to the newborn baby as well…" He added that "It is true that infants appeal to us because they are small and helpless." But he concludes by saying, "If we can put aside these emotionally moving but…irrelevant aspects of the killing of a baby, (then) the grounds for not killing persons do not apply to newborn infants."

Put aside the emotionally moving but *irrelevant* aspects of killing a baby? This is not a guy you want at the Princeton Daycare Center, let alone the Bioethics department.

Source: *Washington Times*, November 9, 2000

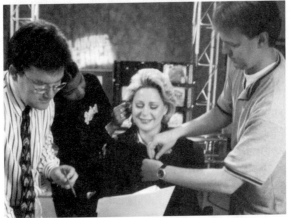

On the TV set with Greg Hoadley, Stacey Mossop (who did my makeup) and cameraman Matt Johnston (who is adjusting the microphone so we can get started).

Left to Right: Rich DeFilippo, Janet Folger, and Jim Carter reviewing a commentary. "What if we say *this*?"

Section 2

Anti-Christian Bigotry

The Father of Our Country proclaimed that religion and morality are indispensable supports for our nation's political prosperity. John Adams said, "Our Constitution was made only for a moral and religious people. It is wholly inadequate for the government of any other."

But you won't find that in any textbook, because history has been rewritten. Historical documents have been altered right under our noses, while we sat by and watched.

The Founding Fathers of the nation, who actually wrote the Constitution, would be surprised to find that they had actually mandated a so-called "separation of church and state." George Washington said, "If I could have entertained the slightest apprehension that the Constitution framed by the Convention, where I had the honor to preside, might *possibly* endanger the religious rights of any ecclesiastical society, certainly I would *never* have placed my signature to it." (Italics mine). In other words, the purpose of the Constitution was to protect Christianity, not attack it.

In a *Coral Ridge Hour* TV interview, Ira Glasser, the executive director of the American Civil Liberties Union, said that the ACLU has done "more for religious freedom" in this country than any other organization by keeping religion "private." They have pushed Christians "into the closet"—especially when it comes to the Christian perspective on the issues of our day.

While there are homosexual writers for most major television sitcoms and 26 homosexual parts on prime time acting as "role models," Christians are routinely portrayed by Hollywood as buffoons and villains. And Christians sit by and wonder why people wouldn't like to "live next door to them," as polls have indicated.

Did you know that Christians used to review and give input into Hollywood scripts? Did they get kicked out? No. They walked away, leaving the void to be filled with those diametrically opposed to biblical views.

Christians gave up the ground; they retreated. They went back to filling their heads with knowledge they will never share—except with Christians in their "separate society" where they know they will be rewarded, rather than ridiculed.

When you read this chapter you will find out that it is later than we think. But while the padlocks are being manufactured to keep Christians out of public square influence, they are not secured on our doors just yet. It's time for Christians to get "out of the closet" and into the public arena and use the voices God gave us . . . while we still can!

Greg's take on the matter.

Pray or Prey?

IN A RECENT *New York Post* editorial we learned that Mildred Rosario, a junior high-school teacher in the Bronx, talked to her students about God.

Peter Melzer, a teacher in the Bronx High School of Science, turned out to be a member of the evil pedophile group called the North American Man/Boy Love Association.

Guess which one is still on the payroll? Mildred was fired. A student asked her if a friend who had recently died was in Heaven? She comforted the students; she also led them in prayer. And for that she lost her job! Peter did not!

Let's see! One prays to God and one preys on boys. Which one do you want teaching your child?

Source: *New York Post*, June 18, 1998

❦

Christians Need Not Apply

IN A RECENT EDITION of the *Village Voice*, an ad appeared for a pair of vocalists that ended with the following sentence: "Must be dedicated, creative, not afraid to offend everyone and anyone. NO CHRISTIANS."

I'm not making this up.

When Catholic League for Religious and Civil Rights President William Donohue tried to place his own ad, replacing the words "No Christians" with "No Gays," the ad was turned down.

The reason given? Bigotry.

It's bigotry all right. The kind of anti-Christian bigotry that is growing more popular on a daily basis. Speak out before CNNA becomes the standard: "Christians Need Not Apply."

Source: Catholic League's *1998 Report on Anti-Catholicism*

Christmas Holiday

TAKE RICHARD GANULIN OFF your Christmas card list. He's the Cincinnati lawyer who filed a federal lawsuit challenging Christmas Day as a legal holiday on the grounds that it violates the First Amendment's guarantee of separation of church and state.

Yet, when you think about it, this lawsuit actually demonstrates that America has always been a Christian nation.

Historically, the state and federal governments of the United States have only observed three religious holidays: Thanksgiving, Christmas, and Easter.

Obviously two of these, Christmas and Easter, are uniquely Christian. And Thanksgiving? Well, that was to God! You simply cannot deny our country's Christian heritage.

Stealing Christmas? Let's leave that to the Grinch!

Source: *American Atheists*, 1998

❧❧

ACLU Curve Ball

Is THE ACLU AGAINST senior citizen discounts—you know, the discounts your grandparents get when they go to the restaurant or hotel?

Well, they just might be headed in that direction.

The ACLU is suing the Hagerstown Suns, a minor league baseball team, because the team offers a discount on Sundays to people who bring in a church bulletin. The ACLU claims this is discrimination based on religion. And the Maryland Commission on Human Relations has agreed.

But the same law that prohibits discrimination based on religion also prohibits discrimination based on age. So when a hotel offers a discount to a senior citizen, are they discriminating?

Come on! The Hagerstown Suns have been thrown a curve ball, and the ACLU should be thrown out of the game.

Source: *American Atheists,* 1998

Aaron Robertson

THE MEDIA HAVE BEEN calling any opposition to homosexuality in any form a "hate crime." But what would they call this?

Meet Aaron Robertson of Westminster, Colorado. A few months back, Robertson and some church friends went to a gay pride parade—not to join in, mind you, but to tell those marching about the biblical truth of homosexuality: that there is hope for change through Jesus Christ.

But as Aaron was exercising his right to free speech, he was assaulted by a homosexual protester, who punched him in the face, leaving him bleeding and in need of stitches. Didn't hear about this in all the hate crime reports, did you? Apparently the media thinks this is a "love crime."

Source: *Colorado Christian News,* August 1998

Michael Eisner

WANT TO HEAR SOMETHING goofy?

Disney Chairman Michael Eisner says that he considers himself a man of moral standards. When NBC's Katie Couric recently asked him how he wants to be remembered, he said as someone with "a strong moral and ethical compass."

That must be a pretty rusty compass.

If nothing else, Chairman Eisner has gone out of his way to insult Christians. Under his watchful eye, Disney subsidiaries have produced films that are violent (like *Pulp Fiction*), and pro-homosexual (like *Priest* and *Lie Down With Dogs*). According to the *Washington Times*, Disney has also fought passage of the "Child On-line Protection Act," which would place restrictions on on-line pornography.

Michael Eisner being remembered for a strong moral compass? That's like Pinnocchio being remembered for telling the truth.

Source: *CultureFacts*, October 7, 1998

✻

Praying Coach Fired

MEET MIKE LIDDELL. UP until a few weeks ago he was coaching a community Little League softball team—that is, until he was fired. Now everyone wants to know what his horrible crime was. Did he try selling illegal drugs to kids? Did he molest them or physically abuse them?

No. No. And no. Liddell did something far worse. After each game he led some of the kids in a voluntary prayer. Liddell had often done that after the game.

But when one parent complained to the League officials, Liddell was relieved of his duties.

Let me ask you something: If he had been wearing a yarmulke while coaching, could one parent have forced him to take it off?

Source: *Fort Lauderdale Sun-Sentinel*, November 8, 1998

Pleasantville

WELCOME TO *PLEASANTVILLE*, THE new movie which tells us that sin brings life (or God in Genesis had it all wrong).

The plot shows two modern-day teenagers who are transported into a world where everything is literally black and white (film is black and white, also). In Pleasantville, the high school basketball team always wins and teenagers go to "lovers' lane" just to hold hands.

As the two teens introduce the townspeople to sin, one by one they turn from black and white to color (on the screen). The kid's stay-at-home mom poses nude and leaves her husband for the artist, and they all live happily ever after.

No mention of the pains of divorce or teen pregnancy or the horrors of abortion. I can't wait for the sequel: *Pleasantville II—Welcome to Reality*.

Source: *Jewish World Review*, November 16, 1998

Bill Press

MAYBE YOU HAVE HEARD that the mainstream media is hostile to Christians. Well, believe it. Bill Press, the *CNN Crossfire* host, recently addressed the Wisconsin Education Association.

Referring to conservative Bible-believing Christians—that would be us—he said, "It's just that their religion is so narrow, and it's so mean, and it's so ugly, and it's so intolerant, and it's so un-Christian."

Let me make a comparison here. Earlier this year the CENTER FOR RECLAIMING AMERICA and other pro-family groups were accused of "hate speech" for saying that there is hope for change for those living in the homosexual lifestyle. Meanwhile, Bill Press says we are mean, ugly, and intolerant.

Is anyone accusing him of hate speech?

Source: *CultureFacts*, November 11, 1998

Starr & Sawyer

DIANE SAWYER'S RECENT INTERVIEW of Ken Starr told viewers a lot more about her anti-Christian views than it did about him.

Among other things, she said people were concerned that his religious principles are "fueling" his investigation of President Clinton. She said, "[People] read that you jog and sing hymns and pray, and they wonder, 'Do you think God is on your side?'"

Sawyer also called Starr "self-righteous" and "sanctimonious," and said, "You certainly have moral certainty in areas where other people have doubt and humanity."

Hmmm. She seems pretty certain of herself. Why is it only acceptable for people on the left—people like Diane Sawyer—to have convictions?

Can you say hypocrisy?

Source: *CultureFacts*, December 2, 1998

Ted Turner

TED TURNER WANTS TO save the world from itself, and he thinks he's just the man for the job. What are his qualifications? He told *World* magazine that he has just two: "I'm rich, and I'm smart."

But when he was asked about how he views world religions, Ted Turner responded that certain Indian religions are good because they worship nature as God.

Christianity, on the other hand, is bad. You see, he blames the Bible for overpopulation because it tells us to be fruitful and multiply. He cites Calcutta, an impoverished Indian city, as an example. Someone forgot to tell Turner that they practice Hinduism there—not Christianity!

Is Ted Turner rich and smart? Maybe he's just rich.

Source: *World*, November 14, 1998

❦

Dartmouth

A YEAR AGO, BILL Bright's Campus Crusade for Christ started an outreach program to the freshmen at Dartmouth College. To each one they gave a copy of C.S. Lewis' classic *Mere Christianity*. A few students protested; but you'd kind of expect that when you send something to 1000 people.

But what happens next is just another example of the selective tolerance that occurs at our universities today: Just as Campus Crusade was set to do it again this year, the Dartmouth faculty tried to stop them. Fortunately, after the incident became public, Dartmouth backed down.

I thought liberals were in favor of the free exchange of ideas.

How long will it be before they start burning the books they don't like?

Source: *Breakpoint*, No. 81222, December 22, 1998

More Trouble in Canada

MATT KINGSWOOD IS A graduate of Knox Theological Seminary here in Fort Lauderdale, Florida. He recently sent us a disturbing news article from Canada.

Kingswood told us of his brother-in-law, Scott Brockie, who owns a print shop. Even though he has several homosexual clients, one day he said "no" to one of them. The reason? He was asked to print literature for a local homosexual group. And as a Christian in good conscience, he could not.

The story doesn't end there. The Ontario Human Rights Commission sent him a notice that demanded a $5000 fine and a written apology! So far Brockie has refused, and in Canada he could go to jail for his firm biblical stand.

You see where tolerance gets you?

Source: *Voices Newsletter,* No. 13, Autumn 1998

Adam and Steve

A NEW PLAY HAS opened in New York based on stories of the Bible. But don't get too excited; this is not *The Prince of Egypt*. It is a spoof of the Gospel from a homosexual perspective entitled *The Most Fabulous Story Ever Told*.

It predictably contains scenes with full frontal nudity and distorts almost all of the major biblical figures. Noah and Moses are gay, of course, as is Adam and his partner Steve. The Virgin Mary is a lesbian, and Christ is the product of artificial insemination.

Don't be fooled. This is not about free speech. This play shows the true motivations behind the homosexual agenda. It's about hostility for the truth of God.

And they say Christians are the ones who are mean-spirited?

Source: *New York Times,* December 15,1998

Impeachment

SO YOU THINK THE battle over impeachment is just political. Well, to hear some celebrities talk, there's a lot more at stake, and what they say is pretty alarming for Christians.

Actor Alec Baldwin commented that "If we lived in another country, we would all right now . . . go down to Washington and stone Henry Hyde to death!" Pretty tolerant stuff.

Alan Dershowitz said, "A vote against impeachment . . . is a vote against fundamentalism, the right-to-life movement, and the radical right. This is truly the first battle in a great cultural war. And if the president is impeached, it will be a great victory for the forces of evil, evil . . . genuine evil."

You realize he's talking about us!

Source: *Washington Update*, December 18, 1998

Bible Quoting Judge

WANT TO HEAR A scary story?

In 1997, 25-year-old Aaron Pattno was convicted for sexually molesting a thirteen-year-old boy. Only he didn't go to jail for it. Why is that?

While sentencing him, the judge read a passage from the first chapter of Romans which condemns homosexuality. Pattno appealed because he said the Scripture discriminated against him. (Never mind that he had committed the horrible crime, the judge's Bible reading made him feel bad.)

The Nebraska Supreme Court heard his appeal and threw out the judge's decision. And just recently, the U.S. Supreme Court refused to hear the prosecution's appeal.

So according to the Supreme Court, it's okay to swear an oath on the Bible; just don't read it out loud in court!

Source: *Reuters*, January 11, 1999

❧❧

CNN & the Church of Satan

THE WEB PAGE OF CNN recently ran a story on the church of Satan and how it has fallen on hard times. Now before you ask why this is news, or rejoice that this organization isn't doing so great, our story doesn't end there.

You see, at the end of the story, the CNN web page has a link to the Church of Satan. When contacted about this, CNN told us that they put the link in "to provide information."

Apparently, CNN thinks it's okay to provide free access to a group whose stated purpose is to bring about evil and destruction into this world and practices magic.

Have you ever seen a link to a Christian organization at CNN? I haven't.

Source: *Reuters/CNN Custom News* (Online), January 26, 1999

The Long Haul

THE BIBLE CALLS FOR Christians to persevere. But are we?

In a recent speech, David Gibbs, president of the Christian Law Association, recalled an encounter he had with an attorney from the ACLU. This ACLU attorney remarked that "Christians are great sprinters, but terrible long-distance runners."

What he meant was that whenever a controversial issue first comes up, many Christians get busy to fight for their beliefs. But after they win initially, the Christians go home and are never heard from again. That is why the anti-Christian forces win as much as they do: they're in it for the long haul, and they know that if they keep trying, the Christians will eventually give up.

For once, I agree with the ACLU.

The Ten Commandments and Sensibility

RECENTLY, FOUR MONUMENTS OF the Ten Commandments were placed in front of four high schools in Adams County, Ohio. Barry Baker, a school district resident, doesn't like them because they are "offensive to his sensibilities." No adultery, no lying or murder?!? I can understand why that might give him problems. So he wants them removed, and as you might expect, the ACLU has taken his case.

With the backing of the Board of Education, Adams County is prepared to go as far as necessary to defend their case.

Cost of defending a lawsuit: about $50,000 so far.

Cost of defending a principle: That's priceless.

Source: *ACLU Press Release,* February 9, 1999

Jesus Kicked Out

THE MINNESOTA HOUSE OF Representatives just kicked Jesus out of the State Capitol. In a 70-62 vote on January 11, the Republican controlled house banned the name of Jesus from all official prayers, ordering chaplains to perform only "non-denominational" prayers. You can say the name of God, but not Jesus.

Apparently they didn't want to offend anyone. Excuse me? I'm offended. Christians in Minnesota are offended.

What right do these men have to censor the name of Him whom we pray to.

Please pray for the people of Minnesota. And by the way, you can use the name of Jesus.

Source: Interview with Minnesota State Representative Doug Reuter

Michelle Shocks

IMAGINE THAT YOU'VE JUST been thrown off a bus for talking about your Christian faith. You might think this could never happen in America.

Well, it did. Meet Michelle Shocks of Seattle, Washington.

While she was riding home, she and a fellow passenger were privately discussing religion across the aisle when the driver asked them to stop. So Michelle then moved to a seat next to the other passenger and they continued discussing their faith. Then the bus driver demanded that they leave the bus at the next stop. So Michelle, who is 25-years-old and 5 months pregnant, was forced to walk the last mile home—in the rain!

Are Christians in the back of the bus? No. Now they're being thrown off the bus.

Source: *Seattle Times,* April 7, 1999

❦

Littleton/Beaumont

TWO SEEMINGLY UNRELATED EVENTS happened last month.

One, in Littleton, Colorado, where two very disturbed teenagers opened fire on their fellow students and killed 12 of them and a teacher. Then they shot themselves.

Meanwhile, in Texas a panel of three federal judges struck down a local public school program. The program invited local church leaders to counsel kids on morality. (You know, the difference between right and wrong?) And according to CNN, the judges were upset that the clergy invited on campus were "disproportionately Protestants."

Where's the connection? Well, kick God out of the classroom and forbid children from being taught right from wrong, and you end up with events like Littleton, Colorado.

Source: *CNN Online,* April 18 & 20, 1999

Drag Queen Bash

EASTER SUNDAY IS A time to celebrate the Resurrection of Jesus Christ. A sacred time . . . but not to the Sisters of Perpetual Indulgence. This group of gay radicals celebrated this day by dressing up in drag as nuns, and throwing a party the size of a city block. The festivities included a "Hunky Jesus" beauty contest, fake nuns dressed in fishnet and heels, and "Pope Dementia."

Does this sound outrageous? IT SHOULD! This blasphemy is the essence of hate speech. Could Christians do the same without any consequences? The answer is obvious. Talk to a person about homosexuality: that's hate speech. Dress in drag and mock Jesus: that's freedom of expression.

Source: *CultureFacts*, March 31, 1999

❧❧

Jesse the Mind

HONORING MICK JAGGER OVER Jesus? That's what Jesse "The Mind" Ventura is doing. A few months ago the Governor of Minnesota declared February 15 to be "Rolling Stones Day," but he refused to sign an order which would have included Minnesota in the National Day of Prayer. Ventura said he did this because, "There are people out there who are atheists. They are also citizens of Minnesota and I have to respect that."

I have a question: Does everyone in Minnesota like the Rolling Stones? By Ventura's logic, that would have to be the case before he could honor them. Jesse's way of thinking doesn't leave much to the mind, and to paraphrase his favorite rock band, it doesn't give me any satisfaction, either.

Source: *Conservative News Service*, May 6, 1999

The U.S. Army Endorses Witchcraft

GUESS WHAT? THE PENTAGON has endorsed "white witchcraft" as an official religion. There are now five U.S. army posts that have witch chaplains. What does this mean? It means that witchcraft, or "Wicca," now has equal standing with Christianity, Judaism, and Islam in the U.S. Army. And guess who is going to pay for Wicca chaplains as they worship "Mother Earth?" That's right, you are!

Who needs Stealth bombers when you have brooms, goat sacrifices, and voodoo dolls?

And do they have to give Halloween off? Is it a paid holiday? It's hard to believe that I'm even talking about this, but I don't think it takes a crystal ball to see that this is a bad idea.

Source: *Austin American-Statesman,* May 28, 1999

Richard Dawkins

IF SOMEONE SAID THAT African-Americans, or women, are like a disease, the outrage would be universal. At least, you would sure hope so.

Yet, people of faith are continually insulted today and few take notice.

Not too long ago the American Humanist Association named evolutionist Richard Dawkins "Humanist of the Year." During his acceptance speech he compared the threat posed by people of faith to "mad cow" disease. So "faith" is like a disease.

He also said that faith is "one of the world's great evils, comparable to the smallpox virus but harder to eradicate."

To "eradicate" means to eliminate or exterminate people of faith. Where is the outrage?

Source: *The Humanist*, Jan./Feb. 1997

PBS Rewrites 1979

WHAT'S THE BEST WAY to ostracize a group of people? That's easy: compare them to known extremists. This just recently happened to Christians on PBS.

That's right. Public television just aired a documentary called "1979: God Strikes Back."

This show reviewed the year of 1979, and it actually tried to link the Islamic Fundamentalism in Iran to Jerry Falwell's "Moral Majority." According to a former TV producer who watched it, linking the two separate movements like this is very easy to do—especially if you have no conscience.

Never mind that the extremists in Iran shot and killed their way into power, while Christian groups merely tried to get out the vote.

And the worst part about it is: you paid for it with your tax dollars.

Source: *National Review Online*, June 29, 1999

The ACLU's War on America

THE ACLU'S WAR AGAINST America continues.

Just recently, a federal judge ordered the town of Republic, Missouri, to alter its official seal. Why? Because it contained the fish symbol that represents Christianity. They said it violated the so-called "separation of church and state." Never mind that the majority of the people wanted it.

It turns out, only one person—a self-described witch, or wicca—was offended by it. And because the ACLU sued on her behalf, one person overturned the will of the people. What about the thousands who were offended by her act? Forget about their values, their heritage, and their voice: a witch is offended.

Source: *Newsday.com* July 14, 1999

You Make the Call

ANTI-CHRISTIAN BIGOTRY JUST scored a touchdown in Denver. The Denver Department of Zoning has issued a "Cease and Desist" order to David and Diane Reiter. Their crime? Holding a Bible study and prayer meeting in their home . . . too often.

What's too often? Try once a week.

The zoning officers said it was a concern over parked cars. But one city official fumbled the ball when he stated that it would be "no problem" if the Reiters were holding a book club instead of a prayer meeting.

So is it OK to have a house full of friends over every week to watch *Monday Night Football*, but not for prayer?

It's not OK! Is the real issue zoning, or anti-Christian bigotry?

You make the call.

Source: *Denver Post*, August 4, 1999

☙❧

Anti-Christian Bigotry, Canadian Style

ANTI-CHRISTIAN BIGOTRY IN Canada has reached a new low. Apparently, Christians are so threatening that the Canadian government now sees them as unfit parents.

Don't believe me? Consider what happened in Quebec recently, when a government employee removed a child from her Baptist family. This bureaucrat did this because she thinks Baptists "might have unusual beliefs regarding child rearing."

Why has this happened? When Christians don't speak up for their beliefs, their basic rights will be taken away. In Canada, that includes the right to raise your children. If we're not careful, children here in America could be next.

Source: *Calgary Herald* August 14, 1999

෴

Rewarding China for Being Evil

TIANANMEN SQUARE, 1989. Who can forget the picture of those brave Chinese students taking a stand for democracy and holding copies of the Declaration of Independence, while their government sent tanks against them?

China has changed very little since then. Christians are rounded up and sent to concentration camps, and millions of women are forced to have abortions every year.

And what is our Congress doing about it? Well, they just renewed China's favorable trade status, by a vote of 260-170. (Maybe that was to reward them for stealing our military secrets.)

So the Chinese government steals from us, persecutes Christians, and forces women to have abortions. And we are rewarding them for it!

Source: *Washington Times*, July 28, 1999

❦

Was Fort Worth a Hate Crime?

IS THERE A DOUBLE standard against Christians in the media, AND in the Justice Department? Well, consider the following. Two days after a man entered a Jewish temple and killed five people, Reno said the shooting was "motivated by hate."

But what do they have to say about the same crimes committed against Christians? Well, a gunman recently killed *seven* people inside a Fort Worth church while shouting anti-Christian slogans. This time, reporters from CNN and CBS suggested "we may never know why" this happened.

Janet Reno now says, "We should not jump to conclusions." Bias from the news media is bad enough. But aren't we supposed to have equal justice?

Source: *Mediaresearch.org* Sept. 23, 1999

ACLU's Double Standard

THE BROOKLYN MUSEUM OF Art has decided to display a controversial painting of the Virgin Mary. But it isn't just any painting: it features her splattered with elephant dung, along with cutouts from porn magazines. Obviously, thousands of people were offended, including the mayor of New York City. He quickly threatened to cut off the Museum's $7 million in funding unless they removed it.

Enter the ACLU. They sent the mayor a letter claiming that his action "is an unconstitutional attempt to censor ideas [he] personally oppose[s]."

How does this hate speech thing work again? Oh yeah: If it's against anyone else, you stop it. If it's against Christians, you force the taxpayers to fund it.

Source: *Jewish World Review*, October 4, 1999

❦

Jesse Ventura & Organized Religion

MINNESOTA GOVERNOR JESSE "THE BODY" Ventura just tried to body-slam organized religion. He called it "a sham and a crutch for weak-minded people who need strength in numbers."

Now because he slammed all organized religion, a spokesman later tried to CLARIFY that Ventura only really meant "Christians." He said that the governor was just referring to those "members of the religious right, who are intolerant, and the Governor hates intolerance."

Oh! If he only slams Christians, that's okay. So Jesse Ventura labels Christians as "weak-minded" and calls their beliefs a "sham" and a "crutch." There's tolerance for you.

Where's the outrage at this "clarification"?

Source: *Associated Press,* September 30, 1999

✌️🕊️

Christians "Cultic" in France

ACCORDING TO *CHRISTIANITY TODAY*, only one half of one percent of France is evangelical Protestant. And because they're a silent minority, the French government now defines evangelicals as "representing extreme factions of the traditional Reformed Church." As a result, the persecution of Christians is growing.

One man was fired from his job because he refused to sign a paper denouncing the church his brother attends as a cult. And government officials just warned a man seeking an appointment to a high office that he wouldn't get the post as long as his children remained in a Christian school.

Isn't the French motto "Liberty, equality and fraternity?" I guess that applies to everyone—except Christians.

Source: *Christianity Today,* September 6, 1999

❧❦

Jesus Poster Censored

FIVE-YEAR-OLD ANTONIO PECK IS our First Amendment Hero of the Month winner. He and his kindergarten classmates were told to create posters about how to protect the environment. So Antonio created a colorful poster with Jesus on it and called it, "The only way to save our world!"

But the teacher told Antonio this was unacceptable. So he created another poster, featuring people picking up trash, with Jesus praying off to one side.

But when Antonio's poster got displayed alongside his classmate's, the part of it with Jesus praying was folded over!

So what does this mean? It means that it's okay for kindergarten kids to make posters about saving the world—so long as it doesn't contain the world's Savior.

Source: Liberty Counsel Press Release, November 1, 1999

Separation of Church & State

TODAY, I'D LIKE TO clear something up: the Founding Fathers did NOT intend to build a wall of separation between church and state. According to historian David Barton, the phrase "separation of church and state" was never mentioned the entire time the First Amendment was being debated by our First Congress back in 1789. (If that's what they wanted, you'd think they would have said something about it, right?)

Also, in the first 150 years of our nation, "separation of church and state" was mentioned less than a dozen times by the federal courts; and that's being generous. During the last 50 years, however, it's been mentioned over 6,000 times.

Who knows best what the First Amendment means—the Founders of our country, or a bunch of activist federal judges today?

Source: Speech by David Barton, October 29, 1999

Is Christianity a Hate Crime?

THIS SUMMER THE SOUTHERN Baptist Convention, representing 15.8 million members, will hold its annual conference in Chicago. Over 100,000 people are expected to be involved in evangelism, housing rehabilitation, work in medical clinics, and church planting.

But the Council of Religious Leaders of Metropolitan Chicago isn't happy. They sent a letter to the Southern Baptists stating, "A campaign of the nature and scope you envision could contribute to a climate conducive to hate crimes."

You've got to be kidding me! The so-called religious leaders are trying to silence the Baptists from sharing their faith. This is actually happening in America, and it is frightening.

Which do you think is the real hate crime?

Source: *WorldNetDaily*, December 3, 1999

༄༅

Congressman McDermott

CHRISTIANS ARE CALLED TO spread the Gospel to all people. But according to Congressman Jim McDermott of Washington state, that's intolerant.

He recently began urging Southern Baptists to end their campaign to convert Hindus. McDermott wrote a letter on congressional letterhead to Southern Baptists and to his fellow Congressmen saying that he could not understand how they "can characterize another religion as spiritually dark and false."

I have a question: Would McDermott be just as angry if Hindus tried to convert Christians? Hindus can try to convert Christians because the First Amendment says they can.

And like it or not, Congressman, the First Amendment also applies to Christians.

Source: *World*, December 18, 1999

❧❧

Jesus Statue Ruled
Unconstitutional

A FEW YEARS AGO, a judge ruled that a statue of Jesus in a Wisconsin public park violated the so-called "separation of church and state."

So a group of concerned Christians bought the area around the statue for more than $21 thousand. That way the statue could stay in the park, right? Wrong! The Seventh Circuit Court of Appeals just ruled that since the statue *appeared* to be on public property, it still violates the Constitution.

So if you live in Minnesota, right on the border with Wisconsin, it may *appear* that you live in Wisconsin. If appearance is all that matters, this judge just might let you vote in both states.

No. It appears to me that the only thing unconstitutional was the judge's ruling.

Source: *CNN Online*, February 6, 2000

❦

Georgetown Censors Writer

ROBERT SWOPE IS A junior at Georgetown University who used to write a column for the campus newspaper. That is, until he got fired.

Why was he fired? Because he criticized an on-campus play that promoted radical feminism and *celebrated* the rape of a 13-year-old girl by a grown woman. Swope wrote of the incident, "Why is rape only wrong when a man commits it. When it's by a woman against a 13-year-old girl, it is celebrated and a university club sponsors it?" Because he spoke out against this, Robert Swope was fired.

So, according to Georgetown University, promoting radical feminism is good. But criticizing it could cost you your job.

Source: *Townhall.com*, March 31, 2000

Prayer OK'd in Capitol

FOUR YEARS AGO, A pastor took some of his congregation on a private tour of our nation's Capitol building. When they were inside, he led them in prayer—that is, until a security guard told them that if they didn't stop praying, they would be arrested. But the pastor was not intimidated. He filed suit to protect his, and our, First Amendment rights.

Earlier this month, a U.S. District Court judge upheld that First Amendment right to pray inside the U.S. Capitol building. Isn't it ironic that they needed a judge to help them decide this? After all, if you look at the large paintings of our nation's founding events inside this same building, you'll find that many of the people depicted there have something in common: They're also praying.

Source: American Center for Law and Justice press release,
April 4, 2000

Tufts University

TUFTS UNIVERSITY IN MASSACHUSETTS has just blatantly discriminated against its Christian Fellowship club. Here's what happened. A lesbian student demanded to be a leader of the Christian group. But she was turned down because the group leaders knew that the Bible teaches that homosexuality is a sin.

So the lesbian student complained to the student government, and in a late-night meeting, which none of the Christians were informed of, the student government revoked all of the Christian Fellowship's group rights.

And guess how the student government notified the Christians of the decision? A voice mail at 12:30 at night. Hey, that's fair.

So according to the student government, either pick a lesbian to lead your Christian group, or get off campus.

Source: *Boston Globe,* April 29, 2000

❦

Ohio Motto Goes to Court

THE 6TH CIRCUIT COURT of Appeals just shot down the motto of Ohio, my home state. The motto reads, "With God, all things are possible," and it's from the Gospel of Matthew.

By a 2-1 vote, the judges decided that the phrase amounts to an endorsement of Christianity, which violates the so-called separation of church and state. Never mind that "separation of church and state" is nowhere mentioned in the Constitution, or that the First Amendment only tells the Federal Congress what they can and can't do. It says nothing about the states.

And that's not all. Guess who sued to have God and the motto removed? A Presbyterian minister. It's bad enough that judges don't know about religious liberty and free speech, but the pastors too?

Source: *CNN Online,* April 25, 2000

Sandia Labs Shows Its Bias

SANDIA NATIONAL LABORATORIES OF Albuquerque, New Mexico, has just blatantly discriminated against its Christian employees.

Here's what happened. A few years ago, homosexual employees demanded that management officially give them special rights, which they did. But when the Christians asked for the same rights, they were turned down. In fact, Christian employees have been told they can't use the company bulletin board, and they've been forced to remove posters and screen savers that have religious content, even family pictures—all because management doesn't want to offend the homosexuals who complained about viewing photos of traditional families.

Discriminating against Christians? That's okay.

Source: *American Family Assocation Online,* May 4, 2000

Constitution Unconstitutional

FEDERAL DISTRICT JUDGE JENNIFER Coffman recently ordered an "offensive" exhibit to be taken down from schools and public buildings in Kentucky. The offense: the mention of God. The documents: excerpts from the Declaration of Independence; the national motto, "In God we trust"; the Mayflower Compact; proclamations by Presidents Ronald Reagan and Abraham Lincoln; and the preamble to the Constitution of Kentucky.

So according to this judge, the Constitution is unconstitutional. As Brian Fahling of the American Family Association said, "This is not just about Christianity; it is about being intellectually honest rather than discarding our true history in favor of a judicial fairy tale."

Source: *American Family Assocation Online,* May 18, 2000

Ten Commandment Book Covers

BACK IN 1980, THE Supreme Court ordered the public schools to take down the Ten Commandments because kids might "read, venerate, and perhaps obey them."

Now a public school teacher has taken that ruling even farther. In a public school near Houston, Texas, a teacher allegedly ordered a student to throw his Ten Commandment book covers away, and called the Ten Commandments "hate speech" that might offend other students.

Another teacher at the same school sent two girls to the principal for bringing their Bibles to school. The principal then threw the Bibles in the trash and said, "This is garbage." Public schools have become more than just religion-free zones; now, they are religious hostility zones.

Source: *World Net Daily,* June 1, 2000

France Targets Proselytizing

IN THE GOSPELS, JESUS tells us to spread His Good News. But the Socialist Party of France wants to make sharing the Gospel illegal.

According to the *Washington Times*, if their proposed legislation becomes law, the French government could shut down a religious group when two or more members are found guilty of proselytizing, and even send guilty parties to prison for up to two years. Those groups include not only Jehovah's Witnesses, but also well-known evangelistic denominations such as Baptists.

The French Justice Minister called this bill a "legal tool to efficiently fight groups abusing [France's] core values." These core values could soon include throwing Christians in jail.

Source: *Washington Times,* June 28, 2000

Russians and Religious Freedom

EVEN AFTER THE COLD WAR, Russian Christians have faced heavy persecution. So in the past decade, over fifty thousand of them have immigrated to America. After all, these Russians came to America to escape religious persecution.

But guess what? The America they were expecting is not the America in which they're now living. For example, they can't believe that their kids aren't allowed to pray in school. According to *USA Today*, one Russian pastor said there is "no excuse" to ban prayer because a few people *might* be offended. And their churches have actually found themselves preaching *against* the American lifestyle.

After all, these Russians didn't expect to face religious persecution in America.

Source: *USA Today,* July 11, 2000

The German Mindset

TROUBLED BY THE COURSES BEING taught in public schools, Johann and Ingrid Harder of Germany began to teach their children at home. According to Johann, "In school, the consciences are being destroyed, but for us, conscience is number one!"

But in Germany, homeschooling is illegal. Harder says, "For weeks we lived like gypsies, getting up early with the … children and studying in the forest. The third time the police came, they caught us at home…." Mayor Hubert Erlichlandwehr authorized the raid on their home arguing that the father should be "temporarily taken out of society" and that the system is designed to produce "a German mindset" that promotes submission to the state.

Could this be like the "German mindset" that led to WWII?

Source: *World*, July 8, 2000

General Mills Says No to the Bible

JUST HOW POLITICALLY INCORRECT has the Bible become?

According to General Mills, the maker of Cheerios and Cinnamon Toast Crunch cereals, the Bible no longer goes with breakfast. You see, General Mills recently started a new promotion, giving away CD-ROM's in their cereal boxes. The problem? The CD-ROM's contained the Bible. Non-Christian and atheist groups complained that giving away free Bibles on CD-ROM's with the dreaded Bible was intolerant. So General Mills announced that they will stop giving away the CD-ROM with the Bible. They also apologized, saying, "Inclusion of this material (meaning, the Bible) does not conform to our policy."

I wonder what it is about the Bible that doesn't conform to policy?

Source: *Detriot Free Press*, July 22, 2000

Will & Grace Intolerance

BACK IN JUNE, I TOLD you how an episode of NBC's *Will and Grace* attacked ministries that help those who struggle with homosexuality and accused them of being "freaks."

So Mike Haley, a former homosexual, wrote to the producers of *Will and Grace* to see if they could discuss their differences. But Jon Kinnally, the executive story editor, wrote back to Haley, mocking him and making homosexual advances toward him, saying "this 'hard-to-get' thing you're playing is Hot, Hot, Hot!"

You see, Kinnally was suggesting that Haley was still a homosexual. Kinnally later told a reporter that "our intention was to make (ex-gays) look like idiots."

Does this sound like tolerance to you?

Source: Focus On the Family Press Release, August 16, 2000

Fort Lauderdale Attacks Boy Scouts

THE CITY OF FORT LAUDERDALE has declared war on the Boy Scouts of America. That's right! By a 3-1 vote, the City Commissioners have stripped funding from a Boy Scout program that helps disabled and disadvantaged inner-city children in high-crime areas.

Hundreds of Scout supporters outnumbered homosexual activists at a public hearing, and phone calls to City Hall favored the Scouts, over two thousand to six. Yet the City Commission voted against the Boy Scouts and the disabled children in favor of the homosexual activists. (Mayor Jim Naugle cast the only pro-Boy Scout vote.)

Please pray for us as we stand to defend the Scouts, our freedoms, and the disabled in Fort Lauderdale.

Source: *Fort Lauderdale Sun-Sentinel*, September 19, 2000

Christian Pedophiles?

IS THERE SUCH A THING AS A . . . Christian pedophile? I hope that even the thought of it is as repugnant to you as it is to me.

But according to *Charisma Magazine*, that's exactly what the Christian Boylove Forum is all about. One of the group's leaders said they were there to help pedophiles who felt God "calling them to be at peace with their current attraction," and that many "see themselves as Christians first and pedophiles second." Can you believe that?

Mike Haley, a former homosexual who now works for Focus On the Family, responded that the Christian Boylove Forum could help people "justify a very sick and detrimental behavior." Woe to those who call evil good, and good evil.

Source: charismanews.com

The Reclaiming America TV Commentary set ...
in position and ready to roll.

Writer Brandon Aronson hacked his way into my
computer day-planner and covertly scheduled me
to buy breakfast for the office. Here he is with
Greg Hoadley and Rebecca Roberts, reaping the
benefits of his computer prowess.

Section 3

Assisted Suicide

In 1976, the Christian philosopher Francis Schaeffer said that once the courts "arbitrarily separated 'aliveness' from personhood," like the Supreme Court did in *Roe v Wade*, what was to keep them from "arbitrarily do[ing] the same with the aged?"

When the pro-abortion slogan "Every child a wanted child" was used to promote the killing of unborn babies who were supposedly "unwanted," it was just a matter of time before that mentality would be applied to our parents and grandparents. While "every grandparent a wanted grandparent" hasn't proven as an effective slogan for them just yet, that same mentality is being used to rationalize the killing of society's other most vulnerable: the disabled and the elderly.

With the exception of Oregon and the Netherlands, society generally tries to talk people down from ledges rather than push them off.

But, if people really *want* to jump, what's the problem? It's not really about suicide. Someone commits suicide every 17 minutes in this country and didn't need any help doing it. This issue is about turning doctors into executioners.

When I debated Jack Kevorkian, I asked him a question. If I was "dumped by my boyfriend, and I didn't want to live any more, would you help me kill myself?" His answer, (at least on the air) was "no." He said he would suggest "counseling." Then I asked him about a similar scenario: if my boyfriend dumped me, and I was feeling alone and vulnerable (as in the example above), but was severely disabled and confined to a wheelchair, would he help me kill myself *then*? His answer? "Yes." In other words, if you are "normal," I'll talk you down from the ledge, but if you're disabled I'll *shove* you off.

And once we give people the "right" to assisted suicide, it is only a matter of time before it becomes their "duty to die." A government report in the Netherlands, shows that over 1000 people annually are killed, even though they had never asked for this wonderful "assistance." I address this in much more detail in *True to Life*. That's the last plug for the book I'm going to make—for now!

You've read about where we are on the issue of killing children; now read on and find out where we are in the killing of adults.

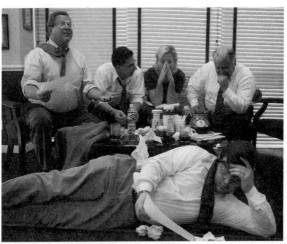

Some days are harder than others!

Kevorkian Body Count

REBECCA BADGER WAS SUPPOSEDLY suffering with multiple sclerosis when she called upon Jack Kevorkian for "help." Turns out, she didn't have MS; she had been misdiagnosed. Now she's dead.

Judith Curren had filed multiple complaints for spouse abuse. Then, the same guy she repeatedly said beat her, took her alive to Kevorkian and brought her back dead. There won't be any more of those nasty reports filed.

Kevorkian has admitted that he wants to "assist" in the suicides of those who are mentally disabled, teenagers, and even the homeless. If one man can assist in the killing of more than 100 people in a state that outlawed assisted-suicide, what's going to happen in Oregon now that doctors have the legal power to kill?

Source: *IATEF Update*

❦

Kevorkian & Reeve

IT WAS THE PERFECT IRONY. On CBS' *60 Minutes*, Jack Kevorkian killed a fellow human being. His victim was a man who thought he had no more hope for living, and nothing left to offer the world.

But listen to what the *New York Post* tells us. Many of the same viewers who watched Dr. Death in action, later clicked over to ABC to watch quadriplegic actor Christopher Reeve star in a TV remake of Alfred Hitchcock's *Rear Window*. Another of Kevorkian's victims was a 26-year-old quadriplegic.

This begs the question: if Jack Kevorkian had offered his services to Reeve just after his accident five years ago, would Reeve have accepted? The question is, do we treat disabled people with compassion, or kill them in their moment of despair?

Source: *New York Post,* November 24, 1998

Taxpayer-Assisted Suicide

AREN'T LIBERALS SUPPOSED TO be compassionate?

In 1997, Oregon became the first state to legalize assisted suicide. According to columnist Nat Hentoff, as of December 1 of this year, if you're poor and destitute, Oregon taxpayers will pay for counseling sessions to verify your desire to die.

But as a spokesperson for the disabled community has pointed out, "The state of Oregon will not fund our [life-saving treatment], yet will pay for us to die."

So what message is Oregon sending? If you're young and vibrant, you live. But if you're old, disabled, poor, or destitute, the state will pay for you to die. And all of this in the name of compassion.

Source: *Washington Post,* February 8, 1999

Youthanasia

A TWELVE-YEAR-OLD CAN'T SEE a PG-13 movie on his own or even drive a car. But in the Netherlands these same twelve-year-olds may soon be allowed to demand assisted suicide . . . and get it!

A new law is pending right now which would make the Netherlands the first country in the world to legalize so called "mercy killings"—even for young children.

A spokesperson for the Royal Dutch Medical Association said, "If the parents don't want to cooperate, it is the doctor's duty to respect the wishes of the patient." Let me put this in plain English: Parents will have no say in the life or death of their own child.

Please pray as if these children's lives depend on it—because they do.

Source: *Associated Press*, August 9, 1999

Rationalizing Suicide

IS ASSISTED SUICIDE RATIONAL or crazy? Well, the *Wall Street Journal* just quoted one advocate who says it is "rational" if the patient suffers from a "hopeless condition." And what might that be? "It includes, but is not limited to . . . a quality of life that is no longer acceptable to the individual."

In other words, assisted suicide advocates believe that suicide is always rational. And 85% of the American Psychological Association members agree. Hey! Aren't these the guys you're supposed to see for help when you're feeling suicidal?

So psychologists surveyed think pushing suicidal patients over the edge is okay!

Call me crazy, but that doesn't sound very rational to me.

Source: *Wall Street Journal*, August 3, 1999

Peter Singer's Dilemma

PETER SINGER, THE CONTROVERSIAL professor at Princeton University, thinks very little of disabled people. He has said that "killing a defective infant is not morally equivalent to killing a person. Sometimes it is not wrong at all."

I wonder if he would be willing to apply that logic to one of his loved ones. As it turns out, Peter Singer's mother now has Alzheimer's disease. But he says "It's different when it's your mother."

Sometimes all you need to do to change a person's mind is to put a human face on the problem. Hopefully, Mrs. Singer's condition will change her son's mind about the value of all disabled people.

Source: *CultureFacts,* September 15, 1999

Assisted Suicide Video

A NEW DO-IT-YOURSELF PROGRAM aired in Oregon, but it's not about cooking or home repair. It's a video guide to committing suicide, based on the best-selling assisted suicide book, *Final Exit*.

Dr. Gregory Hamilton, a Portland psychiatrist and opponent of assisted suicide, said that it tells suicidal people how to be effective. Otherwise, most first-time attempts at suicide fail, giving caregivers a chance to help people through depression. He added that the program promotes "suicide as OK," and, "for people who are on the edge, it pushes them over."

As it is, someone commits suicide every seventeen minutes in this country. Do we really need to promote more suicides?

Source: *Associated Press,* January 31, 2000

Are Hospitals Still Safe?

AMERICAN HOSPITALS USED TO be about protecting the life of patients. But is that still the case? You see, some hospitals now have "futile care" protocols that grant doctors the right to say *no* to *requested* life-saving medical treatment for patients whose lives they consider lack sufficient quality to justify the costs.

In fact, one survey of twenty-six California hospitals showed that almost half of them have policies allowing tube-supplied food and water to be cut off from patients who are in a coma—that is, starve them to death—even against the expressed wishes of the patient and/or family.

So before you go to your local hospital, you may just want to check their policies first.

Source: National Review Online, October 31, 2000

Assisted Suicide in Belgium

It appears that the death legacy of Jack Kevorkian is alive and well...in Belgium. Just how bad has assisted suicide gotten in that small European nation?

Well, it's the cause of death for more than one in ten deaths in Belgium. That's right! According to a recent study, thousands of Belgians are either given lethal injections, or treatment has been withheld with the intention of ending the patient's life, "*without* the explicit request of the patient."

And that's not all: all of these unnecessary deaths are happening in Belgium, even though assisted suicide is illegal! So if you're ever in Belgium, you'd better not plan on getting sick—or better yet, don't go there at all.

Source: *BBC News*, November 24, 2000

Section 4

Education

Some people reading this went to school 30 years ago when the main problems reported by teachers were "running in the hall," "talking in class," and "chewing gum." Now the problems range from "teen pregnancy," "abortion," "drugs," "rape," and "gang warfare." Just look at how far we've "progressed."

When the Supreme Court ordered the Ten Commandments off the classroom walls on the basis that students might actually "obey" them, there was hardly a whimper. Eighteen years later the Court got what it asked for, as students disobey commandments like "thou shalt not murder," and we can't seem to figure out why. *Must be the guns.*

So the Ten Commandments are out, and metal

detectors are in. How enlightened we are.

What's my view of the public schools? Let me put it this way: if your children are in the "government" schools, grab them and run as fast as you can. Enroll them in home school, Christian school, or a private school (in that order), and don't look back. Not a bad action step, come to think about it. I'm kind of surprised it never made it on the air.

This is what I would do, if at all humanly possible, and the good news is we're not limited to what is "humanly possible" because, as the state of Ohio motto reads, "With God *all things* are possible." Teach your children how to lobby; show them how to change the system by speaking at school board meetings, the PTA, and the legislature. In fact, these all make great field trips for any home-schooling family. Perhaps one of their assignments could be to write testimony about what they were once exposed to in the public schools— schools our tax dollars subsidize, no matter where we school our kids.

And what are they exposed to in the government schools? Read this and weep. When you finish crying, stand up and make a difference. Change is possible, and it can begin with you. Bring another parent or two along with you to school and take a look at what your children are learning. See what's in store for the semester, what kind of assemblies are going on, look for the buzz words: "diversity," "safe sex," "safe schools," and programs on "tolerance." Keep reading, and you'll see what I mean.

Last minute edits with Greg Hoadley and Bob Carter.

Greg and Bob kicking back in the studio during taping.

Passing Failures

MASSACHUSETTS GAVE ITS NEW teachers a reading and writing test . . . just to verify their basic skills prior to their being placed as teachers. But an amazing 59% of those college graduates failed the test! (That's 59 out of every hundred for my NEA listeners.)

And the test was designed after the 10th grade test that will eventually be required for graduation from high school!

So what was the state's reaction to this kind of illiteracy among its educators? A crash course in the 3Rs? No. The state lowered the passing grade standard!

How would you feel about their lowering the standard for your heart surgeon or airplane pilot?

They just have!

Source: *US News & World Report*, August 3, 1998

Teen Sex

TEEN SEX ISN'T WHAT it used to be. The Centers for Disease Control is reporting that more than half of the high school students they asked are abstaining!

And it's the first time this decade that the majority of students are saying "no" to sex. The survey also showed that abstinence was almost equal among boys and girls.

So, regardless of what you see in the movies and on TV, teens who are virgins shouldn't feel like outcasts. Despite the media's best efforts, more and more kids are just saying no.

Knowing that God is our Creator strengthens our resolve to follow His operating instructions. After all, He is the One who came up with the whole idea.

Source: *U.S. Centers for Disease Control*, 1998

Nadine Strossen

NADINE STROSSEN, PRESIDENT OF the ACLU, was the keynote speaker at a recent pro-pornography convention in California. She believes that access to pornography should be unlimited, even to children—your children.

So she became very upset when three teen magazines were recently pulled from a public school library in Long Island because of their explicit sexual content.

You see, only the ACLU is allowed to make value judgments. If concerned parents do that, they're practicing censorship; especially if they're Christians.

So should you stand aside, and let the ACLU educate your kids, or should you speak out? After all, who cares more about your kids, you or the ACLU?

Source: *Intellectual Capital,* June 18, 1998

ACLU in Wisconsin

IT USED TO BE that a community could set its own standards. Sure, there might be disagreements about specific standards, but everyone agreed that this was the norm.

This is what a Wisconsin high school did recently. At the urging of parents, the school board banned some pro-homosexual books from the school library.

Enter the ACLU, who is threatening to sue the school board unless they replace the banned books.

Could this possibly be the same group that once forced public school teacher Kenneth Roberts to remove his personal Bible from the classroom, even though he never read it to the students or made them read it?

Does anyone else see something wrong with this picture? Tolerance is definitely a one-way street with the ACLU.

Source: F. Lagard Smith, *ACLU: The Devil's Advocate,* 1996, pp. 151-156

Making College Safe

THE GOVERNOR OF MASSACHUSETTS recently put together a commission whose purpose was to combat alleged discrimination against homosexuals on college campuses. Among other things, they recommended:

1. Mandatory diversity and homophobia workshops for all faculty and students.

2. A gay and lesbian resource center with a paid staff.

3. Campuses must include special housing options for homosexuals, and finally,

4. Any group that opposes the homosexual lifestyle should be strongly discouraged or prohibited from on-campus employment or enlistment recruiting. (That's me and you).

Call the governor of Massachusetts at 617-727-3600. Let him know what you think.

Source: State of Massachusetts, "Making Colleges and Universities Safe for Gay and Lesbian Students"

Abstinence

LISTEN UP EVERYONE. THE tests have been done, the info gathered, and the results are . . . well . . . just what we've known all along: Abstinence education lowers illegitimate births!

The Consortium of State Physicians recently released a report that says abstinence, not sex education, has lowered teen birthrates.

How profound! Instead of educating children and teens on how to take great life-changing risks, we help them avoid them, and it works! As a matter of fact, this study also proved that among the sexually active, teen birthrates have increased!

Thanks to the doctors for showing us what we've known all along: Stay away from the fire, and you won't get burned.

Source: Consortuim of State Physicans Resource Councils,
February 10, 1999

Public Schools & Condoms

I GOT A VERY disturbing letter the other day.

Ron Payson, of Minnesota, wrote to us about a program in his local public schools. In their sex education program, teenagers are given a special assignment: they are to go to a local drug store and purchase a pack of condoms!

I'm not kidding!

Mr. Payson also sent us an assignment sheet for the kids to fill out after the purchase. Among the questions asked were, "How comfortable would you be buying protection here?" and, "Would you recommend that a friend buy protection here?"

Here is my question: Where is the protection for our kids from this kind of garbage. And what's next? Seeing how comfortable our children are when buying pornography?

Source: Letter from Ron Payson, plus homework handouts

Parents Lose in California

ONE OF THE BASIC rights of parents has just been lost in California.

Last September, schoolteacher James Merrick made headlines when he made negative comments about a local minister. The parents of 15 of his students transferred their kids to another class because they were upset about his homosexual activism. That's about half the class!

So what did Merrick do?

He filed a complaint with the district, claiming that he was being discriminated against. Just recently, Chief Deputy Labor Commissioner Jose Millan ordered that those 15 kids be forced to return to his class, against the parent's wishes.

Don't you think parents should outrank a Deputy Labor Commissioner when it comes to deciding what's best for their children?

Source: *CultureFacts*, March 11, 1999

True Love Waits

FOR YEARS, RHEA COUNTY in Tennessee had a bad reputation: it had the worst rate of teen pregnancy in the state. But in the last few years, that trend has changed for the better. What happened?

Meet Cathi Woods. As a Christian and the director of a local crisis pregnancy center, Cathi realized something needed to be done. According to *Christianity Today*, she was a catalyst for change. After getting approval from the school board, she started a new abstinence program for teens. Cathi encouraged open discussion, but she never shied away from telling them the consequences of premarital sex.

In just three years, Rhea County went from #1 in teen pregnancy in the state to #64.

Source: *Christianity Today,* March 3, 1999

❧

Guilty Teacher Missed

IT'S NOT UNUSUAL FOR an assistant principal to call a teacher "a role model for students and staff." But what if that teacher had just pleaded guilty to statutory rape?

Thirty-nine-year-old Lorenzo McCrea, the band instructor at Shaw Junior High School repeatedly had sex with his fifteen-year-old student. He even paid for her abortion!

He was arrested, pleaded guilty, and is in jail. How do the school authorities feel about this? They want him back!

The assistant principal says he is a "role model for students and staff" and that ". . . if there was any way he could return, we would gladly accept him." Just what would he have to do to not be asked back? I know what would do it . . . maybe bringing his Bible to school.

Source: *Washington Post,* June 15, 1999

Right & Wrong Banned

ZACHARY HOOD IS A first grader. His teacher told him that he was so good at reading that he could bring in his favorite story and read it to the class. So, he chose the story of Jacob and Esau (the Old Testament story of two brothers who quarreled and made up). When Zach tried to read it to the class, he was told by the teacher it was inappropriate.

Inappropriate?!? Wait a minute. What if he had brought in *Heather Has Two Mommies* or *Daddy's Roommate* (two children's books that endorse homosexuality)? Would these have been better for the children?

Oh, by the way, Zach's version of Jacob and Esau had no direct mention of God or the Bible.

Absurd, isn't it? Maybe next time they won't accept his lunch money because it says, "In God We Trust!"

Source: *Freedom Forum*, October 9, 1998

❧❧

Beating Up a Teacher

NICOLE SMITH IS A sixth grader in New York who doesn't like getting bad grades. So what did she do when she got a bad report card? She did what any other sixth grader in her position would do—she beat up her teacher—with her mom's help!

According to the teacher, Jamina Clay, mother and daughter took turns: one would hold her down and the other would punch and scratch.

But the worst part is, this type of behavior is now all too common. Even the director of school safety for the United Federation of Teachers was nonchalant: He told the *New York Post*, "We get a few like this every school year when final grades come out."

You know that school discipline has gotten out of hand when the teachers, not the students, get punished for bad grades.

Source: *New York Post,* June 30, 1999

Pedophilia

WHAT'S THE CURRENT STATE of higher education? At Cornell University, pedophilia is in and common sense is out.

It turns out that Cornell is now offering an undergraduate course called "The Sexual Child," which promotes pedophilia. The course objective actually complains that pedophiles are "so stigmatized that it is difficult to find defenders for their civil liberties." Never mind protecting kids from sexual predators; we've got to look out for the self-esteem of perverts.

And the teacher defends the course by saying it's purpose is "to undermine preconceived notions" about children and sexuality.

In other words, common sense is out; child abuse is in.

Source: Accuracy in Academia

☙❧

Traditional Values Harmful

TWO WOMEN PSYCHOLOGISTS AT the University of Michigan have determined that traditional values are harmful. That's right! They are harmful. According to their studies, these values lower the self-esteem of women who believe they are fat. As a matter of fact, they found that believing in the Protestant work ethic or a conservative ideology is also harmful.

Exactly what traditional values or ideology are they referring to? Thou shall not kill? (Obviously very harmful.) Do unto others as you would have them do unto you? (That's just plain vicious!)

The last time I checked, long-standing traditional values had no calories. Neither did a good work ethic.

Source: *US News & World Report,* August 9, 1999

Textbook Travesties

ABC's *20/20* RECENTLY AIRED a special on the numerous mistakes in public school textbooks. And just how bad is this problem? Your kids may have been taught that the first atomic bomb was dropped on Korea. (Actually, it was Japan.) Or maybe they learned that Napoleon won the Battle of Waterloo. (No, it was his biggest defeat.)

And one textbook gave only six lines to George Washington, the Founder of our country, and six pages to Marilyn Monroe!

So what happened to these textbooks? They were recalled . . . and sent to other schools!

So if your children tell you that the Russians were the first to land on the moon, it may not be their fault. There's a good chance they read it in their textbook.

Source: ABC's *20/20*, April 2, 1999, and *New American*,
September 13, 1999

A+ for Easy Cheating

A NEW SURVEY OF public schools shows that cheating is up among students, and even worse, guilty consciences are down. According to the survey, 70% of students said they had cheated in the last year. Of those who had cheated, only 5% have ever been caught.

And how bad do they feel about cheating? Well, not very. One teen put it this way: "Ten minutes of cheating is better than two hours of studying." And another one said, "I feel good that I'm going to get a good grade."

Why is this a problem? Because the students who are cheating today will be building our bridges and performing our surgeries tomorrow.

Well, I guess that's okay, as long as they feel good.

Source: *Insight,* September 20, 1999

✀

CDC Promotes Abstinence?

ATTENTION PARENTS: DO YOU know what the Centers for Disease Control are telling your kids about abstinence?

Well, they have a program called "Reducing the Risk" that they distribute to the public schools. It tells kids who are abstaining from sex that "...you could become a hermit, or [become] so unpleasant that everyone stays clear of you. Or you could never become involved in a romantic relationship."

Did you catch that? The "Reducing the Risk" program teaches that the only way kids can abstain from sex is to become a hermit and be so unpleasant that everyone stays clear of you.

Parents, is this your idea of teaching abstinence? Is this what your child is learning? If you don't know, it might be a good idea to find out.

Source: *Jewish World Review*, Oct. 18, 1999

❦

Teenager Stands for Truth

IS IT POSSIBLE TO take a stand for God in the public schools? Well, if you're being intimidated, sometimes all you have to do is speak up. That's what Kirsys Batista did. Every day for her class reading time her teacher gave her an "F." Why? Because she wanted to read her Bible. (Other kids were reading comic books, and that was okay, but not the Bible.)

Then the teacher threatened to report Kirsys to the principal if she kept bringing her Bible to class. But Kirsys was not intimidated; she visited the principal on her own. The principal told the teacher to stop her bigotry, and the F's suddenly turned into A's.

So what's the lesson here? Don't be intimidated. Do like Kirsys . . . speak up!

Source: letter of testimony from Kirsys Batista

Educational LEGOs

WHAT'S THE LATEST TREND in higher education?

Well, Colorado College, a prestigious private college in Colorado Springs, has abandoned number two pencils and SATs in favor of LEGOs. As part of a new admissions program, potential students get to build a robot out of LEGOs. (And you thought they were just for fun!)

According to the school's Dean of Admissions, "This puts less [emphasis] on the tests that, frankly, have been a stumbling block for disadvantaged and minority students."

My ten-year-old nephew could pass the entrance exam right now!

I don't know about you, but as an employer, that's the first thing I'd be looking for—after finding out what applicants can do with a Mr. Potatohead.

Source: *Denver Post,* February 1, 2000

How to Be Gay 101

US News & World Report recently ranked the University of Michigan as the 25th best in the nation. So what kind of classes are they offering? This fall the school will have an English course called "How To Be Gay: Male Homosexuality and Initiation."

I'm not making this up! The course description in the official fall catalog says, "Just because you happen to be a gay man doesn't mean that you don't have to learn how to become one." The class focuses on teaching students how to be gay by studying drag, interior design, and . . . Broadway musicals!

Interesting. Homosexual activists have been telling us that their behavior is genetic. But now there's an actual course to teach students "How To Be Gay." So, which is it?

Source: *National Review Online*, March 17, 2000

Teachers & Merit Pay

One of public schools' biggest problems is that there is no incentive for teachers to do a better job. No matter how well they do, they will always be paid the same as their peers.

So you would think that public school teachers would be in favor of a system where they get paid more for doing a better job, right? Wrong. Los Angeles public school Superintendent Ramon Cortines found this when he proposed a merit pay system. More than 2,000 teachers protested against it outside his office. Turns out they were afraid they might be paid based on performance.

But apparently, the better teachers were too busy working on their next lesson plan. Who do you think should get paid more?

Source: *Los Angeles Times,* March 29, 2000

New Math

MATHEMATICIANS AROUND THE country and the so-called experts at the Department of Education are divided over the new math courses, which appear to be multiplying in our public schools.

These new math courses, with names like "Mathland" or "Connected Math," invite children to meet in small groups to "discover" math and even construct their own math language. They're based on theories that say correct solutions are not important so long as the student feels good about what he is doing. This led over 200 concerned math scholars, including four Nobel laureates, to denounce these courses.

However, Education Secretary Richard Riley refuses to reconsider. It doesn't add up. Maybe Riley is using new math.

Source: Eagle Forum, March 29, 2000

ACLU on Religion

THE ACLU SAYS THE GOVERNMENT should never endorse religion. But what happens when the religion being endorsed is NOT Christianity?

Two years ago, Arizona Governor Jane Hull issued a proclamation for a "Bible Week," but when the ACLU threatened to sue, she caved in. Well, Governor Hull just issued another state proclamation—that celebrates the birth of ... Buddha.

So what is the ACLU doing now? Nothing. Their spokesperson said, "Although we may think proclamations are inappropriate, they may not violate the Constitution."

So the double standard is official: According to the ACLU, their fabricated separation of church and state applies only to Christianity.

Source: *Washington Update*, May 16, 2000

Public School Tyranny

GERALD AND ANGELA BALDERSON were not happy with the education their child was receiving from the public schools, so they decided to home-school him.

But their school's vice principal had the parents arrested for violating the state's compulsory attendance laws. He had the Baldersons arrested without even checking to see if they had filed the correct paper work—which they had—or even calling them beforehand. As Michael Farris, president of the Home School Legal Defense Association, pointed out, "It is totally inconsistent with Virginia law for an assistant principal to file truancy charges."

I know the public schools aren't crazy about home schoolers, but having them arrested? Isn't that a little extreme?

Source: *World Net Daily,* April 10, 2000

Home-Schooling Success

JASON SCOGGINS IS A 17-YEAR-OLD who recently scored a 1570 out of a possible 1600 on the SAT—including a perfect 800 on the math section.

According to the *Wall Street Journal*, the major reason Jason scored so high is that he was home-schooled. They added that these results are not a fluke: home-schoolers score an average of 67 points higher on the SAT than their public school peers.

But the president of the American Teachers Federation asked, "Why draw any grand conclusions?" Jason's twin brother Jeremy's answer was, "People know that if we've been home-schooled, we'll do a little better than everyone else."

Source: *Wall Street Journal*, February 11, 2000

Church of Satan Visits Public School

What did your kids learn in school today? If they went to Cesar Chavez High School in Washington, D.C., rather than reading and writing, maybe they learned how to sacrifice the family pet. That's because the Church of Satan was invited on campus to share their beliefs with the kids.

But as bad as this sounds, People for the American Way is upset about something *ELSE*. They're angry that the school had parents sign permission slips to let their children hear the controversial speaker, but that no permission slips were required when Christian, Jewish, or Muslim speakers came.

Let me clarify: People for the American Way are NOT upset that your kids are being taught about Satanism. They're upset because parents might find out.

Source: *National Review Online*, June 22, 2000

Parental Rights Usurped

It used to be that school assemblies were for award ceremonies or "pep rallies" to cheer on the team. But a recent assembly at Grand Haven High School in Michigan proved that such gatherings are no longer fun and games, but ways of indoctrinating your children.

School officials held a mandatory pro-homosexual "Diversity Day" assembly. In one seminar students were told that homosexuality was not a choice, and that they were born that way.

Parents were outraged. One parent, Becky Risinger, said, "They took attendance; it was (mandatory), and we knew nothing about it." That's because parental involvement and homosexual indoctrination do not go hand in hand.

Source: American Family Association of Michigan Press Release, June 24, 2000

Ritalin, Public Schools, & KIDS

ACCORDING TO USA TODAY, parents are being forced by the public schools—and the courts—to have their children drugged with Ritalin, a drug used to fight so-called "attention deficit disorder." Some parents have even been threatened with charges of child neglect or abuse and having their child taken away by authorities if they do not give their child Ritalin.

Did you catch that? You could lose your kids by NOT giving them drugs. Whatever happened to "just say no?"

Some parents have solved their child's problem simply by finding a better teacher. Columnist Thomas Sowell suggests, "If legislatures started impeaching judges who punish parents for refusing to drug their children, it would have to stop."

Source: Townhall.com, August 17, 2000

Professor Resigns

RICHARD ZELLER, A PROFESSOR AT Bowling Green University in Ohio, proposed a course exposing the tyranny within academia that forces students to conform to "politically correct" views in order to pass—views like "all whites are racists," or having to write pro-abortion essays, even if one believes abortion is murder.

So what was the reaction to his proposed course? Well, he received death threats and was called "incompetent" and "malicious" by the chairman of the sociology department.

After being treated this way, Professor Zeller resigned. But as he said afterwards, "Don't cry for me. Cry out instead for the students who regularly get intellectually mugged on campus."

Source: *Jewish World Review*, Septepmber 29, 2000

Kindergartners Suspended

YOU'VE GOT TO HAND IT TO the powers that be at Wilson School in Sayreville, New Jersey. You see, they're trying to crack down on crime, which is apparently why they just suspended four kindergartners for three days.

What was their crime? Were they fighting or stealing lunch money? No. They were playing cops and robbers. This was apparently very threatening, because the kids pretended their fingers were guns, and they probably shouted, "Bang, bang," while they ran after the bad guys.

Superintendent William Bauer said, "This is a no tolerance policy. We're very firm on weapons and threats" . . . apparently, even if that weapon is a five-year-old's index finger.

Way to crack down on crime, Mr. Superintendent!

Source: *Court TV Online/Associated Press*, April 6, 2000

GLSEN Targets Kindergartners

ABOUT EIGHT HUNDRED ACTIVISTS, including dozens of teenagers, attended the Gay Lesbian Straight Education Network (or, GLSEN), convention in Chicago.

So what was on their agenda? They have plans to indoctrinate children, beginning in KINDER-GARTEN. Not only that, National Education Association President Bob Chase addressed attendees, saying, "It is an education issue, no matter what the emails (against it) say . . ."

Really. The HIGH SCHOOL STUDENTS in attendance received a "Visitor's Companion" that advertised Chicago's "leather" bars, a sex club and a homosexual bathhouse. Is that an education issue, too? If that's what they're giving high school students, what are they giving to your kindergartners?

Source: *World Net Daily,* October 11, 2000

☙❧

Generous Gift Denounced by Homosexuals

AMERICA ONLINE CHAIRMAN STEVE Case and his wife Jean recently donated $8.35 million to Westminster Academy, a Christian school in Fort Lauderdale.

But what are the Cases getting for this act of generosity? A slap in the face from homosexual activists. The pro-homosexual lobbyist group, Human Rights Campaign wrote the Cases, "Your gift will only create an assembly line of hate and intolerance." You see, Westminster Academy was founded by Dr. D. James Kennedy to promote academic excellence.

So according to Human Rights Campaign, Christian schools produce hate and intolerance. When are Americans going to realize who the real hatemongers are?

Source: *Sun-Sentinel,* October 24, 2000

The Natzification of Student Judicial Procedures at Columbia University

ON COLLEGE CAMPUSES ACROSS America many feminist professors are convincing young women that they are victims of centuries of oppression by men.

For example, take the new student judicial policies at Columbia University. They do away with the principle of "due process" established by our Constitution and resurrect the Star Chamber—a trial in which students accused of sexual misconduct are not even allowed to participate or attend.

Last time I checked the map, Columbia University was still in the United States of America, where the rule of law is still "innocent until proven guilty."

Source: *Washington Times,* October 9, 2000

Section 5

Evolution

Genesis 1:1 says, "In the beginning, God created the heavens and the earth." But if you've been to a public school classroom recently, you might have heard something that sounded more like: "We all came from the primordial slime as the result of one big accident. In fact, you are really nothing more than a complex food processor. There's the bell. Don't be late for your self-esteem class!"

Not only is that not what the Bible says, that's not what science has to say either. As Dr. D. James Kennedy points out in his book, *Why I Believe*, "If you took thin pieces of paper and wrote 1 and then wrote zeros after them, you would fill up the entire known universe with paper before you could ever even write the number. That is how many years it would take to make one living cell." When you think about it, it really takes a great leap of faith to believe that all of this happened by "accident."

For example, take the human eye. If the theory of evolution is true, you would actually have to believe that all by itself, an organism "accidentally"developed a cornea—which is a transparent portion of the body that can allow light to enter into the area near the mind. But in order to function as part of the body, the cornea needs to be made up of living tissue. For that living tissue to exist, this creature would have to simultaneously and "accidentally" develop a system to run the blood through it and bring oxygen and water and immunizations against disease to the rest of the eye ... But that requires blood cells and blood vessels. And that would block the line of sight.

So this creature, now, (according to evolution) "accidentally" develops not only the necessary blood cells and blood vessels for the eye, but "accidentally" develops a special gland that "accidentally" secretes a special fluid that just happens to carry what the blood carries to do all these jobs.

The problem is, fluid on the eye presents another problem similar to what happens when rain gets on your windshield: it blocks your view.

The solution? Something that can act like windshield wipers. Since the transplant liquid needs to be there to do its job, we now need something to "accidentally" develop to evenly distribute the clear liquid across the cornea.

So guess what?

An eyelid "accidentally" appeared, and "accidentally" operates automatically without our having to think about it. And to provide depth perception, a second eye "accidentally" evolves right alongside it at the very same time!

I could go on with this example that demonstrates just how absurd evolution really is, but I think you can see my point clearly—thanks to all those "accidents" that have simultaneously occurred to allow you to read this!

As I said, evolution takes a pretty big leap of faith.

Here's me in the control booth taking a stab at directing the RECLAIMING AMERICA CONFERENCE with John Q, who is holding a note of advice for the cameraman, "I just say 'No!'"

Biology Disproves Evolution

THE THEORY OF EVOLUTION has evolved into fact. Or that's what they would like us to believe. However the problem is that we have more and more evidence to the contrary.

Take the human eye for example . . . pretty complex. You see, 10% of an eye does not give you 10% vision.

For evolution to be possible, a whole bunch of mutations would have to take place all at once. You would need the development of the lens, the pupil, the retina, the cornea, and the brain all together.

If the lens developed without the others . . . no dice. It's a biological impossibility for the lens to reproduce while waiting for everything else to catch up. Biologists call this simultaneous complexity.

Just another biological fact that makes evolution impossible.

Time Miracles

DID YOU KNOW THAT the secret of evolution is time?

In his book, *The Origin of Life*, George Wald stated, "Time is, in fact, the hero of the plot . . . given so much time, the 'impossible' becomes possible; the possible, probable; and the probable, virtually certain. One has only to wait: Time itself performs miracles."

I don't think so.

Evolution is a waste of time and I have a little experiment to prove it.

It is something you can try at home. Have a load of bricks delivered to your back yard. Check on it daily and call me when you see a house beginning to take shape.

Go ahead. Take all the time you want!

Source: Henry Morris, *That Their Words Might Be Used Against Them,* Institute for Creation Research, p. 57

Real Leap of Faith

Have you taken a leap into evolution?

Almost half a century ago, Dr. D.R. Goldschmidt observed that the fossil record did not support the already established theory of evolution.

He, like most scientists, knew there should be literally millions of fossils that show life forms in the gradual process of change. Guess how many he found? None! Zero!

He concluded that instead of gradual change, there must have been a large number of leaps. Just what is a leap? Well, it's like a lizard laying an egg and when it hatches—a bird comes out.

O.K. The theory didn't go over very big then, either. Make sure you have all the facts and that you look before you leap.

Source: Henry Morris, *That Their Words Might Be Used Against Them,* Institute for Creation Research, p. 109

747 & You

DID YOU KNOW THAT a 747 jet is made up of many parts? Some of these smaller parts might seem to be unimportant, but without them, the airplane won't get off the ground.

You see, the 747 was not accidentally formed by a tornado that passed through a junkyard. It was crafted by engineers who took the necessary time and equipment to make the perfect machine.

The same is true of you and me. The human body is made up of extremely advanced cells, which are far too small for the naked eye to see. Microbiologists tell us of remarkably complex structures within these cells.

Complexity cries out design; design cries out designer. Who's the designer? Let's call him God!

Evolution & Probability

EVOLUTION IS A THEORY that says that anything is possible. For example, if you have enough monkeys and typewriters, eventually one of them will type all the sonnets of Shakespeare error free.

O.K. Let's use people instead and try something much easier. Put the letters of the alphabet and the space tiles in a bag. Then have our person spell out "the theory of evolution" with the tiles. If he accomplished a BILLION tries per second, he might succeed once in twenty-six thousand trillion years.

Evolution is not just unlikely, it's improbable. Even a monkey knows that.

Evolutionists Know the Truth

YOU KNOW WHAT'S REALLY amazing about evolution? It's the lack of physical evidence.

Evolutionists study fossils to observe transformations from one life form to another. But the fossil record just doesn't include these transitional forms. Regarding the fossil record, Dr. David Raup of the Museum of Natural History in Chicago says, "The record of evolution is still surprisingly jerky, and we have fewer examples of evolutionary transition than we had in Darwin's time."

That's interesting. Darwin, in his book, *Origin of Species*, said he didn't have any examples of evolutionary transition. Now Dr. Raup says they have less than that. That means they don't have very many!

Source: Henry Morris, *That Their Words Might Be Used Against Them,* Institute for Creation Research, p. 182

Evolution and Ethics

I USED TO THINK that how people behaved had something to do with how their parents raised them. Turns out, I was wrong.

At least that's what evolutionist Robert Wright says in his book, *The Moral Animal*. He suggests that our behavior is determined by evolution, and it's all in the genes. For example, if two parents have strong "fidelity" genes, then their children will be less likely to cheat on their spouse. If not, they're off to divorce court.

In other words, it wasn't Mother Teresa's fault that she loved poor people. She had too many "nice" genes. And don't blame Adolf Hitler for anything he did. He obviously had the "mean" gene.

No. Evolution cannot shape our behavior, because it doesn't exist. But good parents who teach good values can.

Source: *Christian Research Journal,* Spring, 1998

Evolutionary Thought

SCIENCE HAS ALWAYS INVOLVED challenging established theories to find the truth. Unfortunately, some scientists don't think so.

A school board in Detroit, Michigan, recently voted to put some books in the school library that challenge the theory of evolution—books which were written by professors at non-Christian universities.

But the National Center for Science Education went ballistic and demanded that the books be removed. (I'm not sure whether they also demanded that the books be burned.) We can't have any books that challenge the theory of evolution, now, can we?

Thankfully, the school board didn't back down, and today the books that question Darwinism are in the school libraries. Check them out, while you still can.

Source: *AFA Journal,* January, 2000

Evolution & South Dakota

I just got back from South Dakota, and there is a mountain there that proves what evolutionists have been saying all along: That if you just get enough time, wind, rain, erosion and pure chance, anything is possible. You see, this mountain has the faces of four U.S. Presidents on it. It's as if someone actually carved the faces of Washington, Jefferson, Lincoln, and Roosevelt on purpose.

You know, the faces of Mt. Rushmore are no accident. They had a creator. So did the people these carvings represent. Mt. Rushmore didn't just happen. It was designed and created—just like you.

Why Evolution Can't Be True

VICTORY FOR TRUTH IN Kansas. The State Board of Education has just ruled that the teaching of evolution in the Kansas public schools is no longer required

In the past I've told you how the laws of science, probability, and the fossil record all negate the theory of evolution. But some teachers don't want to teach based on the evidence, and according to the *New York Times*, they're threatening to quit if they can't teach just evolution. Isn't education the search for truth? Perhaps these teachers' blind faith and allegiance to evolution prevent them from seeing the scientific evidence to the contrary. The good news is that students no longer have to pledge allegiance to evolution to pass the state test.

Source: *New York Times*, August 12, 1999

Support for Creation

THE LEFT-WING SPECIAL INTEREST group, People for the American Way, apparently tried to put Christians who believe what the Bible says about creation on the defensive. So they commissioned a nationwide poll, allegedly to prove that people don't want creation taught in the public schools.

But guess what? According to the People for the American Way poll, 79% of the American people think creation SHOULD be taught in the public schools. And almost half of the respondents agreed that the theory of evolution is "far from being proven scientifically." Imagine that!

So if the overwhelming majority want creation taught in the public schools, what's stopping them? Maybe it's groups like People for the American Way.

Source: *San Diego Union-Tribune,* March 11, 2000

Another Fake Missing Link

HOW DO SOME SCIENTISTS try to prove the theory of evolution? Sometimes they just make stuff up. Last November, for example, *National Geographic* magazine boasted that they had found a missing link that would prove the theory of evolution. But guess what? It's a fake. Turns out, the animal they discovered was a combination of two distinct animals. It had the body and head of a bird and the feet and tail of a small dinosaur.

But we shouldn't be too surprised. After all, this isn't the first time scientists have supposedly discovered the "missing link" that proves evolution. Every one that has ever been found has been proven to be false.

Once again, what is missing here is real evidence.

Source: *AFA Journal*, April, 2000

Janet's dream world ... "We love you Janet! Let's go through these commentaries again! Have some coffee—we can go another six hours. You're the best Janet!"

The real world .... "Janet, we've been through these commentaries a thousand times already! *They're fine.* Besides, if we hear, '*It needs more punch*' one more time ..."

Section 6

Family

The family is the building block of society. Sadly, groups like the ACLU, Planned Parenthood and People for the (so-called) American Way seek to undermine parental authority, while many states have passed laws that make it easier to obtain a divorce.

Studies also show that children of divorced parents are more likely to engage in pre-marital sex, drugs and crime. So you would think it would be in everyone's best interest to promote the family. David Popenoe of Rutgers University put it this way: "I know of few other bodies of data in which the weight of evidence is so decisively on one side of the issue: on the whole, for children, two-parent families are preferable . . . If our prevailing views on family structure hinged solely on scholarly evidence, the current debate never would have arisen in the first place."

As you will see, across the board, if God says it, real-world evidence will back it up. And once again, God's plan, *His* design for the family, is best for us. Think of the heartache we would save ourselves if we would just listen to Him!

Janet: "What do you think? Should we say *this* instead?"
Chris: "That depends on how many angry phone calls you want to get."

Murphy Brown Revisited

MURPHY BROWN AND DAN Quayle, together at last.

That's right. Candace Bergen, the star of *Murphy Brown* now admits that the former vice-president actually was right on target when he criticized her TV character's decision to have a baby out of wedlock.

According to the *Los Angeles Times*, Bergen said, "It was the right theme to hammer home. I agreed with all of it except his reference to the show, which he had not seen . . . but the body of the speech was completely sound," she said.

I'm delighted to learn of her family values which she maintains she has had all along. Maybe we just couldn't hear it over all the Quayle-bashing.

Agreeing with Dan Quayle now is like Mike Tyson complimenting Evander Holyfield after biting off his right ear.

Source: Media Research Center *Cyber Alert,* June 1, 1998

Polygamy & NOW

IN THE ABORTION DEBATE the National Organization for Women has always stood for what they call choice. But does their position on "choice" now include polygamy as well?

Ellen George, a spokesperson for the Utah chapter of NOW, said yes at a recent conference: "We fight for lesbian families . . . I don't know why we wouldn't support polygamy."

But when the media got ahold of this story, NOW was forced to publicly announce that it had never supported polygamy.

But you've got to wonder, why not? NOW supports lesbian relationships, and favors the killing of children by abortion. So what's wrong with many women sharing the same man? By NOW's logic, it's just another lifestyle choice.

Source: *Washington Times/Claremont Institute*, August 22, 1998

Kids, Parents, and Clinton

IT'S BEEN SAID THAT kids see things in black and white, while grownups see shades of gray.

Is it true? Well, listen to this.

A recent poll by the Nickelodeon TV station asked kids and their parents what the outcome of the recent impeachment trial should have been. And here's what they found: 52% of the kids thought the Senate should have removed President Clinton. But only 40% of their parents agreed.

I think it's because children do see the world differently. Their parents are always telling them not to do the wrong thing, or they'll get punished. So if their president did something wrong, why shouldn't he be punished too?

Maybe on issues of right and wrong, parents could take a little advice from their kids.

Source: CBS *This Morning,* February 19, 1999

Television Fathers

HOW HIGH DO FATHERS rate on prime-time television today? Apparently, not very. According to a recent study from the National Fatherhood Initiative, there are only fifteen reoccurring prime-time fathers on TV. Of those, eleven were either poor role models or uninvolved with their children (like Homer Simpson).

Consider, also, that according to this study there are twenty-five homosexual characters on prime-time network shows.

Did you catch that? Four devoted dads and twenty-five homosexual role models!

What message does this send to the public? That's easy: Gays are good and dads are bad.

Is this what you think? Have you ever told anyone?

Source: National Fatherhood Initiative, March 1999

Ace Alibi

JOHN WATSON WANTS TO provide an alibi for cheating spouses. For as little as twenty-five dollars, his company, Ace Alibi, will provide fake invitations to business trips and phony restaurant and hotel bills, all to cover up for cheating spouses!

Why is John Watson doing this? He says he wants to protect marriage: "I simply don't believe a family should be destroyed over (one night)." He adds, "If someone uses this service, that person obviously wants to preserve [his or her] family."

That's funny. I thought if you wanted to preserve the family, you wouldn't commit adultery in the first place—let alone lie to cover it up. Is this how far we've come?

Source: *AFA Journal*, February 2000

Women Want to Come Home

GERMAINE GREER HAS SPENT her life pushing the feminist ideal: telling women to abandon their traditional role, not have any children, and spend their time climbing the corporate ladder.

But guess what? Greer seems to have changed her mind. She recently said, "I was desperate for a baby, and I have the medical bills to prove it."

And she is not alone. Many other women have believed the lie of feminism for the past 30 years, and they're not happy. In fact, a recent poll found that 68% of three thousand women polled would stay at home to raise the kids if they could.

What does this mean? Seven out of ten women aren't happy with the feminist ideal. I guess it's not so ideal.

Source: *Washington Post*, May 12, 2000,
and *Cosmopolitan*, June 2000

Section 7

Homosexuality

I was speaking to a reporter the other day who asked me why there seems to be a focus on this issue. Why are we not talking as much about other sins? What sets this issue apart from the others is that, unlike most other sins, this is the one that is being forced on us everywhere we turn.

Adultery is another sexual sin about which God doesn't think too favorably. It made a commandment, after all. But as far as I know, there are no "Adultery Pride Parades," and there isn't a group out there pushing to have adulterous affairs subsidized with our tax dollars. And they're not kicking groups out of public schools and parks that disagree with adultery. At least not yet.

While only 1.5-2% of the American population lives in the homosexual lifestyle, a disproportionate amount of time is spent by the mainstream media promoting that agenda. This media tidal wave is in keeping with Marshall Kirk and Hunter Madsen's recommendations in the book, *After the Ball*, in which they advise homosexuals, "First you get your foot in the door, by being as similar as possible. Then, and only then—when your one little difference is finally accepted—can you start dragging in your peculiarities, one by one."

No one can argue about the great gains the homosexual *activists* have made in the last twenty years. How have they done this? I think they have a number of things going for them—namely a sympathetic media, Hollywood, and a passionate intensity unlike most others. You see, to homosexual activists, (not those living or struggling in the lifestyle) their sexual behavior is *who* they are. Any disagreement, it seems, becomes an affront to them and "who" they are . . . as opposed to the behavior in which they engage.

But the thing that I believe has given them their greatest gain is the lack of opposition. That's right! Like a steamroller, they have plowed through the educational system, city councils, county commissions, state legislatures, Congress and the media. And rather than risk getting run over, Christians, just like everyone else, have scurried out of their way.

Don't get me wrong. Being run over is a very real possibility. Just ask Anita Bryant. She stood up to the steamroller and got run over. Ask Senator Trent Lott, football star Reggie White, and recording artists Debbie and Angie Winans. They expressed disagreement with the homosexual agenda and experienced everything from name calling to death threats. There's "tolerance" for you.

These commentaries provide glimpses as to the threat that is out there. I could write a whole book on the subject (and *would* if I thought anyone would read it!). It is the issue that I like dealing with the least, yet it is the issue that poses the biggest threat to our freedoms. Think about it. If they can silence the Boy Scouts for not allowing homosexual leaders to go camping with young boys—like they're doing in my neck of the woods (in Fort Lauderdale)—they can silence those of us who *agree* with the Boy Scouts.

This is an issue that will silence the Church if we let it. If we are going to have a chance, Christians are going to have to be willing to be obedient to God—even in the face of an oncoming steamroller. Because you know what? As unpleasant as it is to be labeled and threatened, we have a God who is bigger than any steamroller, any threat, any group . . . anyone. In this issue, as with all the others, we must trust Him—then obey him. We *must* not lose by default.

You want it *when*?

Bob Carter wasn't available for a photo, so we got a stand-in (actually, a cardboard cut-out) who we took shopping with us.

Cost of AIDS

THE CENTERS FOR DISEASE Control and Prevention released figures in 1996 to show how much federal money (that's your money) was spent per death on the deadliest diseases.

For cancer victims:	$3,776
For heart disease:	$1,056
For victims of stroke:	$765

But for those dying with AIDS and HIV, an astonishing $39,172 was spent per person! That's about 10 times more than the other three combined.

They also report that 65% of men with AIDS were actively engaged in the homosexual lifestyle. AIDS is costing thousands of lives and millions of dollars and is largely preventable.

Source: Focus On the Family, June 1998

Berkeley Boy Scouts

"MEAN-SPIRITED" MERIT BADGES? HELPING ladies across the street based on hate? Berkeley, California, has bid "Bon voyage" to the Boy Scouts of America.

The city council voted 8-1 to end its policy of providing free dock space to a local Boy Scout unit because they adhere to the Boy Scouts' national membership policy which excludes homosexuals and atheists.

Demonstrating both political correctness and intolerance, the city council said, "If we continue to give them the berths rent free, it means government is sanctioning discrimination."

In other words, the Boy Scouts aren't free to be the Boy Scouts. They must follow the homosexual agenda or leave.

So much for tolerance!

Source: *CultureFacts,* August 18, 1998

❦

Gay for Life?

CHECK OUT THE COVER of August 13th's *Newsweek* magazine. It features former homosexuals John and Anne Paulk with the headline: Gay for Life?

The question is a reference to our national "Truth in Love" campaign.

We're continuing to tell the good news that for those trapped in the homosexual lifestyle, there is hope for change.

This issue is touching the hearts of millions around the world. And the members of the press have themselves been overwhelmed.

We've heard from the BBC in London, from Spain, and Australia. And we want to hear from you.

Our full-page ads are available for your church or civic group to place in your local newspapers. This is a critical time to proclaim the redeeming power of the Gospel of Jesus Christ.

Edited by *Nightline*

WANNA KNOW A SECRET?

ABC's *Nightline* is watched nightly by millions of Americans who think they are watching a "live" interview format.

Wrong! And I found out the hard way.

Recently I was asked to appear on *Nightline* in regard to our national "Truth in Love" campaign. On the evening of the broadcast, the "live" segments were taped. Three hours later when the show was televised, I was shocked to realize that several of my answers had been cut!

In the interview, I gave exact statistics showing that homosexual sex is the largest contributor to AIDS. *Nightline* deleted my footnote, thereby giving the clear impression that I was merely stating an opinion.

It makes you wonder . . . what else are they leaving on the cutting room floor?

❦

Salvation Army Attacked

SAN FRANCISCO IS WILLING TO LET the homeless and the elderly suffer in the name of "homosexual rights." The Salvation Army announced that it is being forced to cut $3.5 million from its programs in San Francisco, which requires that all organizations that conduct business with the city are to extend the same medical and retirement benefits to homosexual couples as legally married couples.

The Salvation Army announced it would not bow to the heavy-handed pro-gay policies of the city.

Because of these policies, the Meals-on-Wheels program for senior citizens is being cut. They're also closing down a homeless shelter and an alcohol and drug rehabilitation center—all in the name of "tolerance."

Source: Concerned Women for America, August 3, 1998

Homosexual Misrepresentations

IN THEIR ATTEMPTS TO LEGITIMIZE their behavior, many in the homosexual lifestyle have made some pretty exaggerated claims. The latest: That in 1973, the American Psychological Association determined that homosexuality should be removed from its list of mental illnesses.

But let's look at the facts: Only 16% of the entire APA membership actually voted in favor of the radical change!

And did you know that the vote came about not as a result of new research, but because of militant protests by the radical homosexual group "Act-Up" who used the same kind of lobbying techniques when they stormed St. Patrick's Cathedral.

And as Paul Harvey likes to say, now you have the rest of the story.

Source: Dr. James Mallory, Head of Psychiatric unit — Rapha Center, Atlanta, Ga

❧❧

Newsweek

THE AUGUST 17 COVER STORY OF NEWSWEEK was about the "Truth in Love" campaign and asked the question, "Can gays convert?"

In the September 7 issue, *Newsweek* reports that "nearly 1,000 readers wrote them about the article." However, the real surprise for the editors was lack of controversy. Readers almost uniformly viewed homosexuality as something you are born with.

The fact is that the gay lobby is very well organized, and any time they are subjected to the smallest criticism, their grassroots network is able to come up with hundreds of letter writers. One letter declared, "We need fewer ex-gays and more ex-bigots."

What we really need is fewer silent Christians!

Source: *Newsweek*, September 7, 1998

GLAAD

THE GAY AND LESBIAN ALLIANCE Against Defamation, or GLAAD, doesn't do much to make people happy.

In a report on "anti-gay" web sites, GLAAD conveniently mentioned the KKK and pro-family groups (like the American Family Association) in the same breath. According to GLAAD, all fundamentalists are pretty much the same.

GLAAD is also happily opposed to blocking pornographic web sites at public libraries. Tell that to the parents of the little girl who innocently looked for "dolls" on the internet, and ended up on an X-rated web site.

It is one thing to be against defamation, but for GLAAD to defame others is pretty hypocritical, and their views on free speech leave a lot of people unhappy.

Source: americansfortruth.com

❦

AIDS March

ACCORDING TO THE CENTERS FOR Disease Control, 86 percent of the cases of men with AIDS are males engaging in homosexual sex and/or drug use. How do you avoid catching AIDS? Most of us would simply refuse to take the risks—and if that happened, that would nearly wipe out AIDS. Yet thousands of homosexual activists recently marched in Washington to protest everyone else's alleged bigotry.

What's wrong with this picture? The federal government will spend about $4.7 billion fighting AIDS this year. That's more money than is spent on fighting cancer, diabetes, and heart disease combined.

The best way to stop AIDS? Don't be a risk-taker.

Source: U.S. Centers for Disease Control, 1997

Unabomber

HAVE YOU HEARD THAT CHRISTIANS are to blame for homosexual Matthew Shepard's tragic death? Also, you probably didn't realize that environmentalists are the ones who gave us the "Unabomber."

Both statements are totally false. But which one is the media asking us to believe?

Katie Couric of NBC's Today Show, when talking about our "Truth In Love" ad campaign, said, "It prompts people to say, 'If I meet someone who is homosexual, I'm going to take action and try to convince them or try to harm them.'"

Come on, Katie! There's a big difference between trying to convince someone and killing them. Using that logic, we should punish environmentalists for the unabomber. Right?

Source: *The Today Show, NBC,* October 8, 1998

❧❧

Positive Story

HAVE YOU HAD ENOUGH NEGATIVE stories surrounding the "Truth in Love" campaign? I know I have. Here's a story that will give you hope.

The CENTER FOR RECLAIMING AMERICA was recently picketed by a homosexual man for four days straight.

Towards the end of the fourth day he received a shock: Dr. D. James Kennedy himself came outside to tell him the biblical truth—that there is hope for change for those who want to leave homosexuality.

Dr. Kennedy tells how the man was very hostile at first. But after two hours of discussion, he opened up and showed signs of changing his views.

The next day the man carried a sign thanking Dr. Kennedy for his help. Speaking the "Truth in Love" is what it is all about.

Courage in Canada

CANADA HAS LONG BEEN KNOWN for the Royal Canadian Mounties and the great hockey teams. But nowadays our neighbor to the north may be better known for its "thought police."

London, Ontario, Mayor Dianne Haskett, was recently fined $10,000 for refusing to proclaim a "Gay Pride Weekend." After she lost her case in Canada's courts, she resigned as mayor rather than be forced to proclaim the Gay Pride weekend. She even turned her mayoral duties over to her political opponent—just three weeks before election day!

What do the people of Canada think? Even though she left office and refused to campaign, she was still re-elected with 64% of the vote!

Source: *Religion Today,* October 5, 1998

Homosexual Journalists

OVER 500 JOURNALISTS ATTENDED the seventh annual National Lesbian and Gay Journalists Association Conference in Las Vegas.

Among the subjects discussed was "How to Lobby a Gay Story (and Not Be Dismissed as 'Pushing an Agenda')." (Kids, can you say "propaganda?") During the conference, one attendee asked whether opposing homosexual rights is a legitimate position that should even be printed in a newspaper.

And that's not all. A Florida reporter described Coral Ridge Presbyterian Church as "heinous" for telling homosexuals that there is hope for change.

Letting people know there's hope for change—that's "heinous!" Pushing their own agenda—that's "journalism!"

Source: *CultureFacts*, October 7, 1998

Victims or Liars?

FOR THE PAST YEAR YOU'VE HEARD THE HOMOSEXUAL lobbyists complain about the discrimination they face.

Now I'm not saying this never happens. But as the *Wall Street Journal* reports, some of their claims just aren't so.

Jennifer Prissell of Minnesota claimed to have been beaten while having vicious anti-gay names shouted at her. The police revealed that her story was fabricated.

A graduate student of New Mexico University claimed to have been attacked after her name appeared on an anti-gay hit list. But guess what? She made the list herself, then cut her own arm with a knife to "prove" the attack.

As our "Truth In Love" campaign has been saying for months, let's have a little honesty in the homosexual debate.

Source: *Wall Street Journal,* January 11, 1999

Elizabeth Birch & Family

ELIZABETH BIRCH IS MAKING WAVES AGAIN. The lesbian activist, with her live-in girlfriend, recently adopted twins, a boy and a girl, named Jacob and Anne.

What's wrong with this picture?

According to the National Council on Adoptions, there are thousands of mothers and fathers who have been standing in line to adopt babies for years. They were all overlooked in favor of lesbian political activists.

Also, it just so happens that there is a bill pending in Texas, where Jacob and Anne were born, that would ban homosexual adoptions. A coincidence? I think not!

Jacob and Anne need a mother. They also need a father. But they will be forever denied one because they have become political pawns in the homosexual agenda.

Source: *CultureFacts*, January 13, 1998

❀

Unsafe Sex

TONY VALENZUELA IS PART OF a disturbing trend. He is HIV-positive, and yet he still has random, unprotected sex. In fact, he won't even tell his partners of his affliction unless they ask!

Another man, who wouldn't volunteer his name, has to take 26 pills a day to survive, and he does the same thing. Here's how he justifies it: "In my last days on this planet, I do not want celibacy."

These men are not alone. The Centers for Disease Control reports that 1 in 5 HIV-positive men in San Francisco and New York are engaging in anonymous sex. With stats like these, truth isn't hate speech. It may be the only thing that keeps someone you love alive.

Source: *World*, February 13, 1999

☙❧

Ray Warren

IN MOST CIRCUMSTANCES, Superior Court Judge Ray Warren would be considered irresponsible. After all, this man left his wife and two small children just a few months ago.

But unlike other men in this situation, Ray Warren is considered a hero. Why? Because he left his wife for another man. That's right! After a seemingly normal marriage, he suddenly decided that he was homosexual.

Let's put a little perspective on this sudden change of heart. If Ray Warren had suddenly left his wife for another woman, he would rightly be condemned. But he left her—and their two children—to pursue the homosexual lifestyle. And the homosexual activists are cheering!

But I'll bet his wife and children find his decision out of order.

Source: *CultureFacts,* February 17, 1999

The "Gay" Ugly Duckling

HOMOSEXUAL ACTIVISTS NO LONGER want to be tolerated: Now, they're coming after your kids. Don't believe me? Listen to this.

Openly homosexual actor Harvey Fierstein has created an animated story for children, called "The Sissy Duckling." This is obviously an adaptation of "The Ugly Duckling," but as Fierstein says, "Instead of being ugly, he's a great big sissy."

According to TV Producer Tim Doyle, "There's a group of older people that will never accept it [homosexuality], but there are a lot of empty cemeteries, and when they're filled, the world will be more tolerant."

Translation: "When the parents die, the world will be a better place." Parents, he's talking about you.

Source: *AFA Journal*, March 1999

The Thought Crimes Bill

CONGRESS HAS JUST INTRODUCED something called the Hate Crimes Prevention Act. It sounds harmless enough, but what's really going on here? Well, homosexual groups are using the tragic deaths of Matthew Shepard and Billy Jack Gaither to try to get it passed through Congress.

But here's a little taste of what we can expect if they succeed. David Ott, a former homosexual, came across a pro-homosexual demonstration and got into a discussion with a protester. As a result, Ott was charged with a hate crime, ordered to attend sensitivity training, and incurred over $7,000 in legal fees.

Thought police and re-education centers? Is this what we want for America?

Source: *Coral Ridge Hour* interview with David Ott

Homosexuals Influencing Public Education

HOMOSEXUAL ACTIVISTS SAY THEY'RE not trying to recruit your kids in the schools. But what do the numbers say?

Well, San Francisco has arguably the most pro-homosexual schools in the nation. But that won't affect the numbers of homosexuals, because they're born, not made, right? According to an article published in *Time* magazine, 18% of teens in San Francisco either claim to be homosexual or are "questioning" their sexual orientation. That's nearly 20%. Compare that to the national average, which is as low as 3% of all U.S. teens.

The numbers speak for themselves. I ask you: do you know what your kids are learning?

Source: *AFA Journal*, May 1999

NYPD Recruiting Sado-Masochists?

WHAT'S THE MAIN REASON for having a police department? Well, to protect law-abiding citizens. So wouldn't it be in the police department's own best interests to try and recruit respectable, law-abiding citizens?

They're not doing that in New York City. Their police department has begun recruiting at street fairs for sado-masochists! Let me clarify: that's an openly homosexual celebration of violent and perverted sex.

When asked why they want to recruit people who practice perverted sexual acts, an NYPD representative said they can't "discriminate," and "just because they use whips in their beds doesn't mean they can't be good police officers."

We used to tell our kids that if they get lost, go find a policeman. What do we tell them now?

Source: *Lambda Report Online*, July 11, 1999

Coming Out for Intolerance

HOMOSEXUALS TELL US THAT tolerance is at the center of their movement. Their slogans are "live and let live" and "freedom for everyone."

Apparently, this applies to only those who agree with them. On National Coming Out Day, the American Family Association hosted an open discussion on homosexuality. How did the crowds respond? Well, when former homosexual Michael Johnston was giving his speech on how homosexuals could change, he was greeted with a blueberry pie in the face.

And when Jerry Falwell said (via satellite) that homosexuals were free to leave the lifestyle, phrases like, "Christian bigots get out of our city!" were shouted. Think the goal of homosexuality is tolerance? Think again.

Source: *San Francisco Chronicle*, October 11, 1999

College Homosexual Dance

ATTENTION PARENTS! Would you be concerned if your fourteen-year-old was going to a college dance? And what if this was a dance for gays and lesbians? Well, this is exactly what happened at Everett Community College in Washington State.

The campus hosted a conference called "Links and Alliances '99" for homosexuals aged fourteen to twenty, which featured a dinner and dance. State Senator Val Stevens wrote a letter to the college president saying, "I am very concerned that public funds are being used to enable possible solicitation of sex to children as young as fourteen and adults as old as twenty."

Be on the lookout for Links and Alliances at a school near you.

Source: *The Oregonian,* October 18, 1999

Salon Magazine

THE ONLINE MAGAZINE *SALON* sent writer Dan Savage to work undercover as a volunteer for then-presidential candidate Gary Bauer. Savage hates Bauer's belief that homosexuality is a sin.

Savage had just gotten sick with the flu, and he bragged in his column that he wanted to "get close enough to Bauer to give him the flu." So Savage wrote that he coughed on everything—even licked pens and doorknobs, hoping to spread his flu virus.

So far, the mainstream media has little to say about Savage's column, and *Salon* has not taken any disciplinary action against him. Imagine the mainstream media's outrage if a Christian journalist had done this to a pro-homosexual candidate.

Source: *Salon,* January 25, 2000 and
New York Post, February 1, 2000

Homosexual Recruit Video

HERE IN AMERICA THERE'S A VIDEO called *It's Elementary* that promotes homosexuality in our public schools.

But listen to what they're doing overseas. A video called *Beyond a Phase: A Practical Guide to Challenging Homophobia in Schools*, has just been distributed to schools all across England. In this video, a boy tells children that they should "try experimenting with both boys and girls to see who you feel most comfortable with."

How long will it be before public schools in this country start showing something like this to your kids?

This just goes to show: The homosexual movement is not about tolerance; it's about forcing their agenda on a captive audience and recruiting innocent children into a dangerous lifestyle.

Source: *The Journal* February 1, 2000

No Limits on Showtime

SHOWTIME, THE CABLE TV CHANNEL, has started a new ad campaign called "No Limits." And that's the perfect title when you consider what they want to show you.

In an interview with *TV Guide*, director Joel Schumacher says he wants to adapt a homosexual British soap opera called *Queer as Folk* for Showtime. The show features the intimate lives of homosexuals in England, and it has included sex scenes between a 29-year-old and his 15-year-old boyfriend.

Is this the kind of program you want shown on your TV? More importantly, do you want your kids watching this? Showtime says "No Limits." Maybe we ought to tell Showtime "No way."

When you call to cancel, tell them why.

Source: *TV Guide,* January 20, 2000

CDC & Homophobia

HOMOPHOBIA IS A LABEL HOMOSEXUAL activists have given to those of us who believe what the Bible says about homosexuality—that it's a sin you can turn from and find forgiveness for. But in a recent Centers for Disease Control report, they listed social and economic factors like poverty, unemployment, and (get this) homophobia as risk factors for HIV infection.

Let me be clear. According to the CDC, not only are Christians homophobic, but they are responsible for spreading AIDS. You've got to be kidding.

Robert Knight, of the Family Research Council, concluded, "If [Christians] don't pick up on this, churches could lose their tax exempt status, and mere opposition to homosexuality could be a hate crime."

Source: *World Net Daily,* February 7, 2000

Victory in California!

VICTORY IN CALIFORNIA! The voters of our nation's largest state overwhelmingly rejected homosexual marriage.

Homosexual activists pulled out all the stops trying to defeat Proposition 22, which would keep marriage the way it's always been—between one man and one woman. Not only did they call it "divisive," they actually persuaded the California State Attorney General to change the name of the initiative from "Definition of Marriage" to "Limit on Marriage," to make it sound discriminatory.

But the voters of California weren't fooled. They realize that marriage as we know it has been successful for thousands of years, because God designed it that way. Congratulations, California, for taking a stand for marriage!

Homosexual Superheroes

EVERYONE KNOWS THAT COMIC BOOK heroes have long fought for truth, justice, and the American way. But now, there's a new category: homosexual rights. That's right! A division of DC Comics has just introduced two new comic book heroes: Apollo and Midnighter. But they aren't your average superheroes. You see, they are homosexuals who live together.

In the comic the characters are seen kissing and are hailed as the world's finest couple.

Why is this a problem? Remember the outrage over Joe Camel? Everyone knew this cartoon character was bad because he pushed cigarettes on teenagers. Shouldn't there be just as much outrage against DC Comics for pushing homosexuality on teenagers?

Source: *Sunday Times* (U.K.) February 27, 2000

Repealing Family Values

IN 1988, THE BRITISH PARLIAMENT passed a law known as Section 28, which prohibits the promotion of the homosexual lifestyle in schools. But now Parliament is attempting to repeal that law and permit homosexuality to be promoted in the schools.

According to *USA Today*, most people, including head teachers, don't want the law repealed. Cardinal Thomas Winning, head of Scotland's Roman Catholics, said, "I will not stand for this type of behavior which is now being described as wholesome and healthy, when it is far from it." He added, "What pains me about this whole situation is that the silent majority are so silent that the silence is deafening. I wish they would speak up for their society."

How about you? Are you speaking up?

Source: *AFA Journal*, March 2000

Sexual Fingers?

IS SEXUAL ORIENTATION DETERMINED by . . . the size of your finger? Well, according to a study in *Nature* magazine. This hands-on study—no pun intended—apparently found that homosexuals have shorter index fingers than heterosexuals.

How was this study conducted? According to Knight-Ridder News Service, participants in a pro-homosexual parade in San Francisco were interviewed, and xerox photos of their hands were taken. So much for the scientific method. These researchers had an agenda to push.

Let's put our finger on the real problem. As thousands of former homosexuals prove, homosexuality is not genetic, and bogus studies lose to the truth, hands down.

Source: *MSNBC-Online*, March 29, 2000

GLSEN Pushes Homosexuality

THE GAY LESBIAN STRAIGHT EDUCATION Network (GLSEN) wants to indoctrinate your kids. At a recent conference in Boston they held a workshop that was open ONLY to kids aged 14 to 21. According to a sworn affidavit, children at this workshop were taught how to perform grotesque sexual acts on each other.

And that's not all. The three adults who ran the workshop were all homosexuals who were on the Massachusetts Department of Education payroll. So guess what? If you live in Massachusetts, this is what your tax dollars are paying for. And it was all sponsored by the Gay Lesbian Straight Education Network.

Is GLSEN active in your school district? You might just want to find out.

Source: MASSNEWS, June 28, 2000

NBC Slams Former Homosexuals

WHAT'S A GOOD WAY TO WIN an argument when the facts are against you? That's easy: just ridicule your opponents.

This is what the NBC show *Will and Grace* did in an effort to discredit Christians and former homosexuals. In a recent episode, a homosexual character went to an ex-gay meeting, where he successfully seduced the group leader and exposed the former homosexuals as hypocrites.

You see, the pro-homosexual producers of *Will and Grace* can't fight the fact that thousands of men and women have successfully left homosexuality behind.

On ABC's *20/20*, John Westcott recently said, "Some people hate us because if we're living the truth, then they're living a lie."

Source: Focus On the Family press release, May 3, 2000

Another Bad California Bill

IN THE PAST YEAR, I've warned you about some of the dangerous bills that have been introduced in California to support the radical homosexual agenda. AB 2142 is the latest to pass the state Assembly. If this bill passes the state Senate and becomes law, it will be illegal to discriminate against someone based on their perceived gender.

In plain English, this means you would be breaking the law if you refuse to hire a cross-dresser, transvestite, or drag queen.

Christians in California just voted overwhelmingly to defeat homosexual marriages in March. But in the last general election, they didn't turn out to vote for their state representatives. Hopefully, this November, they can correct that mistake.

Source: leginfo.ca.gov, April 4, 2000, and Traditional Values Coalition *Action Alert*, May 16, 2000

Cross-Dressing Student

SEVENTEEN-YEAR-OLD BRIAN PETERS occasionally wore pink lipstick, carried a flowered purse, and sometimes wore a T-shirt that said, "Sorry Girls, I'm Gay."

But it wasn't until he slipped into a black lace blouse, a long skirt, and a filled-out bra that he got into trouble. Naturally, the teacher sent Brian to the principal's office. He was then suspended when he refused to change his clothes.

Linda Jessell, from the school district office said, "We can restrict student expression and dress when it disrupts the learning environment for other kids." And so says the Supreme Court.

But Brian responded, "The message they're sending to students is that I am not normal, that I am disruptive, that I am wrong."

Yeah, Brian. I think that is what they're saying.

Source: *The Oregonian*, May 3, 2000

Victory for the Boy Scouts

THE U.S. SUPREME COURT overturned a New Jersey Supreme Court decision that had imposed the homosexual agenda on the Boy Scouts of America.

You may have heard that this was about discrimination, but it was really about the Boy Scouts of America being forced to retain a homosexual activist as a Scout leader. After he [the homosexual Scout leader] was dismissed, he then sued the Scouts, who believe that homosexuality is immoral and take an oath to be "morally straight." The New Jersey Supreme Court reinterpreted the Scout's oath for them.

The Supreme Court decision vindicates the Scouts in their battle to both set and interpret their own guidelines. This decision is a victory for the Boy Scouts, for families, and for freedom.

Source: Boy Scouts of Amercia, et al, v Dale, June 28, 2000

Ann Landers Gives Bad Advice

HOMOSEXUAL ACTIVISTS SAY THAT Dr. Laura is controversial because she tells the truth about homosexuality.

But compare what Dr. Laura says about homosexuality to what professional advice-giver Ann Landers says. A concerned parent recently wrote Ms. Landers, telling her about a little boy in her daughter's pre-school class who had long curly hair and wears dresses and stockings like a girl. This parent asked Ann Landers if cross-dressing might hurt the boy. So how did Ann Landers respond? She said, "Wearing girls' clothing and playing with dolls will not make the boy gay," and she told this parent to mind her own business.

So according to Ann Landers, there's nothing wrong with parents sending their pre-school boy to school wearing a dress. And Dr. Laura's controversial?

Source: *Fort Lauderdale Sun-Sentinel*, June 7, 2000

GLSEN Targets Christians

BACK IN MAY I TOLD YOU THE Gay Lesbian Straight Education Network (GLSEN) indoctrinated kids at a public education conference in Boston. Children as young as 14 were taught how to perform grotesque sexual acts on each other.

But there's more. The same conference also held a workshop for teachers on how to combat the . . . "Religious Wrong." (I guess that's you and me.) GLSEN's Leif Mitchell compared Christians to Nazis and had participants think of ways to oppose them at the local level.

But when one teacher questioned whether such tactics might silence the free speech of Christians, Mitchell responded, "There is no argument. We are right and they are wrong." Parents, he's talking about you.

Source: *MASS News,* June 28, 2000

Coca-Cola Changes God's Original Formula

REMEMBER "NEW COKE"? That's when Coca-Cola decided to change its original formula. Executives hoped that their customers would accept the new formula, but instead they rejected "New Coke." The company almost went bankrupt before switching back to the original recipe.

It seems that Coca-Cola has not learned its lesson. They just announced that the company has decided to change another time-proven formula— God's formula for the family. Coca-Cola has decided to extend benefits to same-sex domestic partners.

I encourage consumers to reject this "new formula" for the family, and demand that Coca-Cola revert back to the original recipe—a loving relationship between one man, and one woman. . . . NOW THAT'S THE REAL THING!!!

Source: Human Rights Campaign, June 2000

Homosexuals in the News Rooms

IS THERE A PRO-HOMOSEXUAL BIAS in the news media? Richard Berke, the national political correspondent for *The New York Times*, recently addressed the National Lesbian and Gay Journalists Association. He told his audience that "there are times when . . . literally three-quarters of the people deciding what's on the front page are not-so-closeted homosexuals."

Well, that explains why most Americans know who Matthew Shepard is, but have never heard of Jesse Dirkhising. When Shepard, a homosexual, was murdered two years ago, it made national headlines. But when two homosexuals murdered 14-year-old Dirkhising, the media ignored it.

A pro-homosexual bias in the news media? Even *The New York Times* says so.

Source: *Accuracy In Media*, June 9, 2000

Problems with Hate Crimes

IS THE MEDIA INVENTING a hate crime epidemic? Arthur "J.R." Warren was brutally beaten to death by two teenagers in rural West Virginia. A front-page story in the *Washington Post* insists that his death was a hate crime—that J.R. was killed because he was black, homosexual, or both.

But buried in the story was the possibility that Warren was killed by his homosexual lover. This was only briefly mentioned, and the *Post* story didn't follow up on it. You might think this is an important part of the case, but the possibility that J.R.'s alleged murderer was his homosexual lover doesn't fit into the pro-hate crimes agenda now, does it?

You see, they're too busy using this story to spread the myth of a hate crime epidemic. Is the media doctoring our news? You be the judge!

Source: *Washington Post,* July 20, 2000

NAMBLA—Sued for Murder of Boston Youth

THE NORTH AMERICAN MAN BOY Love Association may soon become the defendant of a class-action lawsuit involving any of the "thousands of children raped by NAMBLA members each year."

A Boston attorney has filed a $200 million lawsuit on behalf of Barbara and Robert Curley. Their ten-year-old son, Jeffrey, was raped and murdered by two men who, according to the Curleys, were given "the last bit of courage needed to kill Jeffrey" from visiting NAMBLA's website at a Boston library. The lawsuit charges NAMBLA with "encouraging its members to rape male children, and providing an underground network for pedophiles."

Finally, the families of children victimized by NAMBLA can take action.

Source: *Conservative News Service*, July 17, 2000

GLAAD Lies About Homosexuality

WHAT'S THE BEST WAY TO WIN an argument when the facts are against you? You make stuff up. That's exactly what the Gay and Lesbian Alliance Against Defamation (GLAAD) spokeswoman Cathy Renna did when she declared that "The scientific evidence that we can point to states that [homosexuality] is genetic."

They then pointed to the American Psychological Association web page for proof. But guess what? The APA web page contains no such evidence. And a spokesperson for the APA responded, "We have NOT said it's genetic." The *Washington Times* added, "...no study has ever been able to prove that homosexuality is inherited."

No. Homosexuality is NOT genetic, and quoting made-up studies won't change that.

Source: *Washington Times*, August 1, 2000

APA Condemns Pedophilia-phobes?

MEMBERS OF THE AMERICAN PSYCHOLOGICAL Association gathered at the Washington Convention Center for a major conference.

According to the *Wall Street Journal*, these mental health experts gathered to "condemn the B-1 Bomber, vilify Dr. Laura, and . . . (get this) . . . actually suggest that Americans have in inordinate fear of pedophilia (or child molesters)." During the conference, an APA program made reference to "pedophilia-phobes."

So the APA says if you're against homosexuality, you're a homophobe. Now, if you stand against child molesters, you're a pedophilia-phobe. See the trend? Maybe they're the ones that should have their heads examined.

Source: *Wall Street Journal*, August 11, 2000

The Pedophile Professor

A FEW YEARS AGO, Hollywood made the movie *The People vs. Larry Flynt*, and turned the infamous porn hawker into a First Amendment hero.

So who does Hollywood want to celebrate as a hero on film now? Alfred Kinsey. Back in the 1950's, he was the guy who told the world that ten percent of the population was homosexual, that "healthy and intelligent" people use pornography, and that children enjoyed being molested. (By the way, his studies have since been refuted.)

Let me be clear about this. Alfred Kinsey is the man who set the stage for the '60s sexual revolution by coming up with outrageous and untrue claims about human sexual behavior, and now Hollywood wants to celebrate him as a hero.

Source: *World Net Daily,* October 25, 2000

Greg hard at work.

"No, not those *little* pizzas; I say we get two *large* pepperoni's."

Section 8

Inspirational

In the Sermon on the Mount, Jesus called us to be salt and light. This may seem hard for believers today, especially with the assault against Christianity so prevalent. Christians need to be reminded that yes, we are on the winning side. After all, Jesus Christ won the greatest battle of all when He died for our sins on the cross and rose again. Psalm 2 reminds us that God is actually *laughing* at those who plot against Him! Since God's Word is truth (John 17:3), we have no need to be afraid. As Romans 8:31 says, "If God is for us, who can be against us?"

As you read about what's going on in the world, remember, "Do not be overcome by evil, but overcome evil with good" (Romans 12:21). And don't forget, "He who is in you is greater than he who is in the world." (1 John 4:4). You get the idea.

LA Times

JAMES LAMBERT IS A SPORTS FAN, but as he read the *Los Angeles Times* sports section, he was disgusted with the numerous advertisements for adult businesses—you know, for massage parlors, adult clubs, and escort services. (Does anyone really believe they are just escorts?)

So he decided to sit down and write a letter. I know what you're thinking . . . "Big Deal!" But would you believe that he received a reply that said "not only are we not going to run them in the sports section anymore, we are not going to run such ads at all!" The letter was personally signed by the president and CEO of the *Los Angeles Times.*

What one person can do is phenomenal!

Source: Interview with James Lambert

Silver Dollars

HAS ANYONE EVER ASKED YOU why Jesus was so special? Well, statistically, He's unbeatable. He fulfilled hundreds of prophesies in His lifetime, and few people seem to understand the significance of that. Let me paint a picture for you.

Cover the entire state of Texas with silver dollars two feet deep, and put a red "X" on just one of them. Blindfold someone, and then give him one chance to pick it.

Sound impossible? That's because it is! Did you know that these were the odds of Christ fulfilling just eight prophesies?!? And He fulfilled over three hundred.

The next time someone asks you why your Creator is so special, give them a reason. The odds are good they'll understand!

Resurrection Evidence

HOW MANY EYEWITNESSES WOULD IT take to convict a bank robber? Would 5 or 10 be sufficient? I would think so.

Now, if I asked you how many eyewitnesses would be needed to prove the Resurrection of Jesus Christ, you would obviously need a large number of people to confirm such an important event in history. So how many were there? The Apostle Paul wrote in 1 Corinthians that there were over 500 eyewitnesses—most of whom were still alive when he wrote his letters. He also said that if the Resurrection never happened, then our faith is worthless.

Five hundred eyewitnesses? Sounds like an open and shut case to me.

The Reliability of Scripture

WHY DO CHRISTIANS CALL THE BIBLE the Word of God? Among other things, it is very reliable and consistent. However, skeptics point out that since we don't have the original manuscripts, how do we know that the New Testament Scriptures are reliable?

The answer is that over 24,000 copies were made of the New Testament letters and spread across the Roman Empire. No documents of any other religion, historical figure, or ancient author can compare to this.

Put this into perspective. There are only 49 existing copies of any of Aristotle's writings. Yet why is it no one questions whether Aristotle actually authored any of his writings? The answer is that the New Testament expects something of you, and Aristotle doesn't.

The Norwegian Miracle

CAN A CHRISTIAN RUN for office on biblical princi-ples and win? Seems unlikely, but amazingly, that's just what happened.

Kjell Bondevick, a Lutheran pastor and father of three, decided to run for the office of Prime Minister of Norway (like running for president here). He announced he was running and was laughed at. Initially, he only had 7.5% of public support, yet he continued his campaign. His posters read, "Pray for our nation. Pray for our election." On September 15, Bondevick won and today his approval rating is an incredible 92%.

If it can happen in Norway, it can happen here.

Source: *Breakpoint,* February 12, 1998, No. 80212

❦

Prayer in the Mississippi News Room

IT'S BEEN SAID THAT RELIGIOUS liberty no longer has a prayer in the public forum. Well, it does on WMDN-TV in Meridian, Mississippi. Let me explain.

WMDN General Manager Marc Grossman decided something positive needed to be done to counterbalance the Littleton tragedy. So he started a segment called "Keep the Faith." At the conclusion of the news broadcast, local pastors from all denominations will be invited to give a short commentary and prayer.

Grossman said he is doing this because he hopes to effect positive change in even the smallest possible way. He said, "We believe in prayer. We believe our community is calling out for prayer."

Do you think your local news station might be interested in doing that? Why don't you let them know?

Source: Conservative News Service, May 14, 1999

Life and Death Faith

THE NEWS HAS REPORTED yet another shooting of Christians. This one in a Fort Worth, Texas, church. But there is more to the story:

According to *World* magazine, nineteen-year-old Jeremiah Neitz refused to lie on the ground when the gunman began firing. Instead, he sat in a pew and began praying. After a few moments, Jeremiah walked up to the killer and said, "What you need is Jesus Christ in your life."

Astonished, the gunman stopped and sat in a pew. Jeremiah said, "Sir, you can shoot me if you want. I know where I'm going—I'm going to Heaven."

That's when the shooting stopped. The name of our God is powerful. If you don't believe me, just ask Jeremiah.

Source: *World,* October 9, 1999

Madalyn Murray O'Hair

CHRISTIANS REMEMBER MADALYN Murray O'Hair as the woman who led the movement to remove prayer from public schools.

Just four years ago, she disappeared with $600,000 she allegedly pilfered from her atheist followers. Just recently, O'Hair's remaining possessions were auctioned off by the IRS to pay for her back taxes. Items sold off included a Bible (yes, that's right, a Bible) and her diary. Six times in her diary, there was a sentence that read, "Somebody, somewhere, love me."

What does this tell us? It says that sometimes the most angry and bitter people are the very ones who are hurting the most. They are in need of our love.

Source: *Christianity Today,* March 3, 1999

Greg: "Jan, take a look at this, here's something *no one* else has reported yet. *We'll scoop them all!*"

Here's how Chris normally looks, along with Barry Kase, lining up television and radio stations coast to coast.

Section 9

Pornography

As we look at the issues of the day, take a look at pornography. Well, don't *look* at pornography—but you get what I mean. Think about it. God's plan for your life is for you to have someone wonderful who will love you for the rest of your life—in good times and bad, in sickness and in health. Satan's plan is for you to look at someone you can never have that could care less about you. *Great deal.* Sign me up. It's really a colossal rip-off when you think about it. Yet people are falling for it by the millions every day and paying more than $50 billion every year in this country to get ripped off.

Americans spend more money per year on pornography than they do on Major League Baseball, National League Football or the National Basketball Association. According to *Adult Video*

News (a publication of the pornography industry), there has been no better time in American history to be a pornographer. Obscenity prosecutions slowed to near extinction under the Clinton administration, and adult-industry output has doubled in the last five years.

I'm going to be meeting with Attorney General John Ashcroft in a few weeks to see if we can go about reversing this trend.

Psalm 101:3 says, "I will set nothing wicked before my eyes."

Why does this issue matter? Read on.

Our TV crew: from left to right Augie Slaven(sound), Rose Mas, Matt Clover (Engineer), Paul Barber (lighting), Matt Johnston (camera), John Quarquesso (director). Without them we would only be on radio.

The Probelm of Pornography

IN 1996, AMERICANS SPENT OVER $8 billion on pornography, including phone-sex, cable programming, and computer porn. This kind of pornography has more than quadrupled in the last 10 years.

Pornography—a "victimless crime?" A study of sex offenders found that 86 percent of convicted rapists said that they were regular users of pornography, with 57 percent admitting direct imitation of pornographic scenes in the commission of their rapes.

What can you do? Oklahoma City closed 150 sexually oriented businesses and saw the number of rapes decrease 26 percent, even though it increased in the rest of the state.

Get the facts . . . before pornography affects your family.

Source: Oklahoma State Bureau of Investigation, Rape Statistics - Oklahoma City vs. Balance of Oklahoma, 1983-1988

Internet Porn

COULD PORNOGRAPHIC MAGAZINES soon be available for checkout at the public library? Don't laugh; it could happen.

Heidi Borton was a librarian for over 10 years. One day at work a fourteen-year-old boy called and asked her if he could look at nude pictures on the internet at the public library. She had no choice but to tell him yes. The library allows that. So the boy asked the next logical question: If the library would let him look at hard-core pornography on the internet, then why didn't they also subscribe to pornographic magazines?

The librarian eventually resigned her position rather than become a panderer of pornography.

Internet smut is out there, and it's legally accessible to kids at the public library. Can porn magazines be far behind?

Source: *Filtering Facts*, 1998

❦

Loopholes

THE FAMOUS COMIC, W.C. FIELDS, was once seen reading the Bible. When a passerby asked him why he was reading it, Fields replied, "I'm looking for loopholes."

A loophole is an ambiguity in the law that provides a means of evasion.

As I'm speaking, pornography shops in New York City are using loopholes to stay in business. These shops are classified as "adult entertainment," which the mayor is trying to shut down. So guess what the porn industry is doing about it? They're now saying that they will allow children into their facilities—if accompanied by an adult. After all, if they let kids in, they're no longer just for adults, right? And the New York State Court Judge, Stephen Crane, agreed!

What's next: Porn shops offering family discounts?

Source: *CultureFacts*, November 18, 1998

Renting Pornography

THE ACLU IS DEEPLY CONCERNED. One of our nation's liberties has been threatened, and they are on the case. Are they defending the rights of the defenseless unborn for a chance to live? Not hardly! They are defending something much more important—your right to rent pornography.

That's right. The ACLU sent a threatening letter to Ohio prosecuting attorney Alan Mayberry. What was his offense? Mayberry had notified local adult video store owners that they could be subject to obscenity prosecution.

Rest comfortably, America! The unborn may perish, and you may be arrested for praying in your schools, but none of that matters to the ACLU as long as you can rent your pornography.

Source: ACLU Press Release, January 13, 1999

Internet Porn and the Workplace

IF YOU'RE AN EMPLOYER, what do you expect from your employees while they're on the clock? Well, you might just expect them to work.

Apparently, the ACLU doesn't agree. Let me explain.

A federal judge recently upheld a Virginia law which forbids state employees from looking at pornographic web sites while working.

The ACLU lawyer, who valiantly fought for the state workers' right to view pornography on the job, was bitterly disappointed. He said the decision "warps the general rules for when public employees are entitled to free speech protection."

So let me get this straight. The ACLU says it's "warped" to expect state employees to work and not look at pornography on the job.

Source: *Associated Press*, February 11, 1999

Wesleyan School Promotes Pornography

JOHN WESLEY WAS A GREAT Christian, and the founder of today's United Methodist Church. Years after his death, his followers founded Wesleyan University in his honor.

But it's a good thing Wesley didn't live to see what's become of the school that bears his name. Just recently, the president of Wesleyan University, in Connecticut, ordered a review of a course there entitled "Pornography: Writing of Prostitutes." One course requirement is that the students produce their own work of porn. Students were also required to read academic critiques of *Hustler* magazine.

John Wesley has been slandered. If the University decides to keep the course, maybe they should rename the school. I have an idea: how about Larry Flynt University?

Source: *The Courant*, May 8, 1999

❦

Covering Up An "R" Rating

WHEN YOU'RE AT THE MOVIES, what's the difference between an R and an X rating (which has been renamed NC-17)? According to the Motion Picture Association of America—about 65 seconds.

That's how much time was edited in the new Warner Brothers film, *Eyes Wide Shut*, to bring it down to an R rating. Sixty-five seconds! And not one scene was actually cut. Computer graphics were used to block out the most blatantly sexual images.

Afterwards, actress Nicole Kidman said, "Thank God not a frame was cut—and that's so important to us."

So if you think your kids are now safe to go to an R-rated movie, just remember, they might be only 65 seconds away from seeing an X-rated film.

Source: *USA Today*, July 16, 1999

Public Library Pornography

IN A PORTLAND, OREGON, public library a shocked parent observed a child watching a pornographic web site. She brought this to the attention of a staff member who responded, "We don't restrict access to material here" and "you shouldn't be looking over someone's shoulder."

The New York public library's Internet policy, guided by American Library Association statements, says that the library "does not limit access to materials or attempt to protect users."

Really? Guess how many of the almost 9,000 public library systems would give *Hustler* magazine to your 10-year-old? None.

You see—they already do limit access—and they should. Library Internet protections are long overdue.

Source: *Filtering Facts*, September 10, 1999

Good Porn

In November of 1998, Ronald Thiemann, dean of Harvard Divinity School, resigned. It was discovered that he was downloading and viewing pornography on his office computer. (That's the head of the seminary!)

Harvard Law Professor Randall Kennedy thinks that's not so bad. He said, "Some church services can be beautiful, uplifting, and memorable. The same can be said of certain pornographic films, writing, and painting."

Let me get this straight: According to a Harvard Law Professor, porn is the same as a good church service? PLEASE!!!

Is it any wonder that we have the problems we do, when this is the view of those who train our pastors, lawyers, and congressmen?

Source: *Intellectual Capital,* July 15, 1999

Omni Hotels

HOTELS CAN BE DANGEROUS places for families nowadays. I'm talking about the pay-per-view pornography they offer. Stay at any hotel and a single man or woman can watch so-called "adult entertainment"—for a price. And when you check out of the hotel, it's usually billed under "anonymous charges," so no one will ever know.

But there's good news. Omni Hotels, one of the largest chains in America, has decided to drop this filth. While they expect their bottom line to decrease as a result, their vice president of marketing said, "Not all business decisions should be fiscally driven. We believe this is the right thing to do."

So if you're doing some traveling in the near future, you just might want to consider staying at Omni.

Source: Omni Hotels press release, November 4, 1999

It Takes Two to Tango

VLADIMER CHACON-BONILLA RECENTLY received an 18-month jail sentence. He had a sexual liaison with an 11-year-old girl that he met on a chat line on the Internet. The girl's mother discovered this man in her little girl's closet with his pants around his ankles.

However, Judge Durke Thompson didn't think that crime was so bad. He said, "This was very intrusive and disruptive and harmful, but it has not wrecked anyone's life." He added, "It takes two to tango." State Attorney Doug Gansler said, "This was not a tango. This was sex between an adult and a vulnerable little girl."

Internet filters can protect your children from chat rooms like this, but you'll need to vote to protect your children from judges like this.

Source: *CNN Online*, January 6, 2000

Internet Sex With Seven-Year-Old

ACCORDING TO THE *CHARLOTTE Observer*, a man offered his 7-year-old daughter for sex on the Internet—by using terminals at a public library and free e-mail service. The incidents occurred from June until October of last year.

The man was found out by his estranged wife, not the public library. As usual, the public library claims no responsibility. But wait a minute. Even convenience store clerks are responsible for not selling cigarettes, alcohol, or pornography to minors. Why can't we expect the same from public libraries?

Librarian David Burt said, "How many more children have to be exploited like this before the American Library Association changes its immoral, indefensible policies?"

Source: *Charlotte Observer*, December 24, 1999

Victory in Erie, Pennsylvania

VICTORY FOR FAMILIES AND local communities! The U. S. Supreme Court has just upheld an ordinance in Erie, Pennsylvania, that bans nude dancing. In their 6-3 decision they ruled that local and state governments can, in fact, have standards of decency. What a concept!

But some people are not happy about this. In his dissent, Justice Stephen Breyer called the decision a "bad precedent," and the *New York Times* editorial page called the Court's decision "disappointing."

Guess what? Stephen Breyer and the *New York Times* writers don't live in Erie, Pennsylvania. But there are lots of families who do live there that will now be protected from sexually-oriented businesses by this decision.

Source: Family Research Council Press Release, March 29, 2000

ALA Approves of Internet Porn

BACK IN MARCH, THE Family Research Council released a report of "over two thousand documented incidents of patrons, many of them children, accessing pornography...in public libraries."

And according to an internal American Library Association memo, that's a good thing. ALA governing council member Mark Rosenzweig wrote in this memo, "adult ignorance (and) attempts to contain the curiosity of kids is bad." He added that the ALA should be "sex-positive. . . . We should not make children ashamed of their sexual curiosity on the Internet or in literature," and he suggested that children *should* be exposed to graphic sex, including bestiality.

So forget the triple-X porn shops. All your kids really need is a library card.

Source: *World Net Daily,* October 20, 2000

Section 10

United Nations

How far out in left field is the United Nations?

According to a report by the Heritage Foundation, UN Committees have "expressed concern that parents in England and Wales were *allowed* to withdraw their children from sex education programs in school." Not only that, they "advise countries that prohibit prostitution to legitimize it, and countries that have relaxed their laws against prostitution to extend to prostitution all the legal rights afforded other professions." The expectation of "having children" is a "negative stereotype" or "obstacle" that girls face as they try to advance in society.

They are also worried that parents may pass harmful values to their children. (I wonder if by "harmful" they mean things like "those pesky Ten Commandments and biblical beliefs?")

And that's just the tip of the iceberg.

Not only are they anti-family; their spokespersons include such stalwart intellectuals as Sharon Stone and a former Spice Girl; they say there are too many people in the world (in spite of the evidence to the contrary); and to top it all off, they don't want Christians to share their faith with others. In his book titled New Genesis, longtime UN member Robert Mueller declared his dream of establishing a one-world church. But there's just one problem: those darned Christians. So how does Mueller propose dealing with this problem? He wrote, "Peace will only be possible through the taming of fundamentalism."

If you believe what the Bible says, he's talking about "taming" you. George Orwell's *1984* has nothing on the UN. Take a look at what I mean.

Sharon Stone

SHARON STONE, AN EXPERT ON sex education? The United Nations seems to think so. Stone told a UN panel discussion on AIDS that, "No matter how much we guide our children within our families and within our churches, we are not stronger than the power of sexuality."

And her solution? Condoms, condoms, and more condoms. She says all parents should keep a box of 200 condoms in the house where teenagers can find it. That way, teens won't be embarrassed about what they do, and the parents won't know.

Hey, while you're at it, why not put a box of 200 clean needles where your kids can find it, because of the power of drugs. And why not a box of a couple hundred cigarettes while you're at it?

Sharon Stone, UN expert? Right!

Source: *Associated Press*, December 2, 1999

No Spanking

THINK THE UNITED NATION'S influence doesn't affect you? Think again! The United Nation's Convention on the Rights of the Child proposes that Congress, not parents, be the national guardians of your children (Article 3).

As a direct result, this type of thinking is being exercised on local fronts as well. A Christian boarding school, known as Second Chance Ministries, was raided by 25 armed officials from the Colorado Attorney General's Office and Sheriff's Office. There had been allegations of child abuse. As it turns out, the only "crime" that was committed was paddling for breaking school rules.

The U.N. just moved into your back yard.

Source: Rutherford Institute, September 13, 1994

❦

Spice Girls Speak for the United Nations

THE UNITED NATIONS. A few months ago they invited actress Sharon Stone to speak for them in a panel discussion on teen sexuality. Stone recommended (with a straight face) that parents supply their teenagers with boxes of 200 condoms.

Guess who's speaking for the United Nations now? Former Spice Girl Geri Halliwell.

Apparently singing "If You Wanna Be My Lover" makes you an expert on sexuality.

In fact, she's doing so well that she almost got booted out of the Philippines, a predominately Catholic country.

Over five billion people on the globe, and the UN picks a Spice Girl to represent them. I wonder who their next spokesperson will be—Madonna? Or maybe Monica Lewinsky is free?

Source: *Newsday,* June 15, 1999

Myth of the Population Explosion

THE UNITED NATIONS RECENTLY complained that there are now more than six billion people in the world. They say the world is getting too crowded and that there is no longer enough food for everyone.

But is world population a serious problem? Not really. As Stephen Moore points out in *National Review*, "Enough food is now grown in the world to provide each [person] with almost four pounds of food per day."

And as for lack of space, you and your 6 billion closest friends could all comfortably fit into the state of Texas. There is enough space there for each family of four to have a house and one-eighth of an acre of land.

And if Texas gets too crowded, we might have to spill over into Oklahoma—but you get the picture.

Source: *Jewish World Review*, October 19, 1999

❦

UN and Mother's Day

THE UNITED NATIONS WANTS TO do away with all forms of discrimination against women. According to the *Wall Street Journal*, the UN found that the former Soviet Republic of Belarus is guilty of "fostering the continuing prevalence of sex-role stereotypes."

What was Belarus' crime? They celebrate Mother's Day. That's right! Don't they realize that it's discriminatory to show appreciation to your mother? (I hope you haven't sent her that card yet!) After all, the United Nations knows better than we do . . . right?

No. The organization that's out of touch here is the United Nations. The UN wants to be our mother. But as Belarus knows, there's no substitute for the real thing.

Source: *Wall Street Journal*, March 17, 2000

UN Takes Aim at Christians

THE UNITED NATIONS WANTS TO bring about world peace by silencing Christians. According to *Insight Magazine*, delegates at the UN's Millennium Peace Summit of Religious and Spiritual Leaders were told "that religions need to accept the validity of all beliefs to attain world peace."

And Episcopal Bishop William Swing, who may soon head this movement, said that in order to achieve this peace, proselytizing "will not be tolerated." That means sharing the Gospel and fulfilling the Great Commission . . . WILL NOT BE TOLERATED.

I wonder how they plan on enforcing this? Are they looking to put offenders in jail? If you're a Bible-believing Christian, they're talking about you.

Source: *Insight Magazine*, October 2-9, 2000

Section 11

Miscellaneous

One of the cool things about being a Christian, besides having your sins forgiven and being assured a place in Heaven, is having a road map for life. God has spelled out what is best for us, and if we will follow it, we're going to be the bene-factors. And no matter what subject we happen to be looking at, if your position is based on what the Bible has to say about it, you're going to be right. That's a pretty cool thing.

Whether it's abortion, pornography, gambling, or homosexuality, God's way is best. And the real-world evidence is going to bear that out. Doesn't matter what it is. And it doesn't matter what the "politically correct establishment" thinks. There is a God. He has a plan. And His plan is best.

Gambling—You Bet Your Life

DR. JAMES DOBSON JUST finished serving on the Federal Gambling Commission. He has found that there is a direct link between gambling and divorce, child abuse, and domestic violence. He concludes that "gambling ruins lives and wrecks families."

And the numbers back him up. According to the Commission, over 30% of gamblers are either pathological or "at risk."

And the industry preys on the most vulnerable, like the young and poor. Americans spend more money on gambling than groceries, and the number of "Gamblers Anonymous" chapters in America has doubled since 1990.

Some people might say they can handle a little gambling, but I wouldn't bet on it.

Source: Focus On the Family, July 1999

❦

The Police State of Connecticut

According to our Constitution's Second Amendment, you have the right to bear arms.

But the state of Connecticut has just passed a law which "allows confiscation of a gun before the owner commits an act of violence." That means that if your neighbors know you own a gun, they can force you to turn it in if they think you might commit a crime!

The law also requires that law enforcement officials keep detailed files on these so-called "dangerous" citizens who actually believe in the Second Amendment. This would include an inventory of gun ownership, psychological, and perhaps political profiles as well.

So if you own a gun to protect your family in Connecticut, this law is aimed at you.

Source: *New American*, August 16, 1999

Christians & Culture

The doctrine of tolerance says that all belief systems and truth claims are equal. But are they?

The great Princeton theologian, J. Gresham Machen, didn't think so. He once wrote, "False ideas are the greatest obstacles to the reception of the Gospel." Why? To paraphrase him, if all religions are seen as equal, fewer people will come to know the truth of Jesus as their Savior.

And guess what? A new Gallop Poll shows that Machen was right: North America is now the only continent in the world where Christianity is not growing.

No . . . tolerance should never come at the expense of truth.

Source: *Princeton Theological Review*, 1913

Bill Clinton & Sex Trafficking

Every year, over 2 million women and children around the world are forced to become prostitutes. And if President Clinton gets his way, prostitution will become a legitimate business.

According to an article in the *Wall Street Journal*, the White House has been pushing the United Nations to narrow its definition of "sexual trafficking." If they're successful, they would create a loophole in international law that would say prostitution is legal if these women and children "consent" to selling their bodies for sex.

No. Children don't consent to becoming prostitutes, and women shouldn't be encouraged to become trapped in it. Nor should the President of the United States help pimps promote prostitution as a legitimate business.

Source: *Wall Street Journal*, January 10, 2000

Final Commentary

We've been doing the "Reclaiming America" commentary for two and a half years now, to bring you a Christian perspective on today's issues.

But in order to concentrate full-time on grass-roots activism, I'm sorry to say this is our final commentary. I'd like to thank everyone who has contributed to our efforts, including the five hundred radio and TV stations who aired our commentaries daily. Thanks, also, to the National Religious Broadcasters for giving us their Genesis Award . . .

. . .which is why we have put the best ones in this book for your reference. Thank you again for listening, and God bless you.

Section 12

The Writing Process

I was interviewed by a reporter from the *Cleveland Plain Dealer* a few years back and asked, "What is it that you do?" My answer? "Think up stuff and do it." I explained that my quote was "off the record," but, of course, it appeared in the article nonetheless. One of the things I thought up was the idea of a daily radio commentary. Not the most original idea; there were plenty of commentaries from plenty of people on plenty of stations. But I wanted these to be a bit different. This is the commentary that launched our television debut:

> Ted Turner wants to save the world from itself, and he thinks he's just the man for the job. What are his qualifications? As a recent *World* magazine article quoted him, he has just two: "I am rich

and I am smart." But when asked about how he views religion, Turner responds that certain Indian religions are good, because they worship nature as God.

Christianity, on the other hand, is bad. You see, he blames the Bible for overpopulation, because it tells us to be fruitful and multiply. He cites Calcutta, an impoverished Indian city, as an example. Someone forgot to tell Turner that they practice Hinduism there, not Christianity!

Is Ted Turner rich and smart? Maybe, he's just "rich."

You miss something without hearing the delivery, but I think you get the point— maybe he's "just rich."

Some thought that perhaps this wasn't as nice as it could be. Their point was well taken. It's not really something I would say at a dinner party where I might have a chance of changing someone's mind: "Excuse me sir, but you're just not too bright." However, when a public figure makes hypocritical statements flagrantly bashing my beliefs—I believe I'm free to expose that hypocrisy, even if the person being exposed might not care much for the idea. And, rather than coming across as angry, isn't it much better to use a little humor to make the point?

In fact, probably the most often-heard words in commentary review process were, "It needs more punch." Facts alone are pretty stale—you might even say . . . boring. I wanted these to be relevant, fun, and easy to remember and use. And, if at all possible, provide action steps for Christians to make a difference. That's a pretty tall order for a commentary with less than a minute to make a point.

I've been asked to provide a little insight into the Commentary writing process. I guess so people don't feel ripped off when they buy a "commentary book" with just commentaries! So let me give you just a few examples. One technique I would often incorporate was to try and take an absurd situation that was happening in the news to the next logical step to show just how ridiculous it really was. For example, about two years ago Sharon Stone told a U.N. panel that she thought parents should just give their teens boxes containing hundreds of condoms because, in her words, the "power of sex" is just too much for any teenager to handle. (Yes, she really said this!) So, in the commentary I suggested that while we're at it, why not give kids hundreds of filtered cigarettes, because of the "power of cigarettes"—right? And parents? Better provide your kids with hundreds of clean needles—because of the "power of drugs!" Great idea. And while you may miss it without hearing the delivery, *that* would be sarcasm!

But a problem with that method arose that I couldn't have anticipated in writing and recording these in just three years time. Things got so absurd that there was no *next step* to take! For example, a teenaged boy in Massachusetts was suspended from high school for dressing like a girl and using the girl's restroom, after repeatedly being told not to. You know—the kind of problems our *parents* experienced in school!

After awhile we toyed with the idea of ending every commentary with the words, "I'm not making this up!" There was so much going on that was so far out there that I sometimes felt like the "*National Enquirer* of Christian radio commentaries." Take a look at this one that couldn't make it on the air:

> "Feminism has reached an all-time low in parts of Europe and Australia. According to reports in the *English Spectator*, a new movement has begun in parts of Sweden, Germany, and Australia to force men to sit down while they are urinating! A feminist group in Stockholm University is campaigning to ban all urinals, and a

Swedish elementary school has already removed all its urinals. Why in the world would some feminist women demand such a foolish thing? Well, according to the *English Spectator* report, "a man standing up . . . is deemed to be triumphing in his masculinity, and by extension, degrading women." Others have said that standing up is a "nasty macho gesture" and if women can't do it, men shouldn't do it either!"

Unbelievable. And I'm not making this up! *See what I mean?*

But writing the commentaries wasn't always fun and games. Although there were things to laugh about in every session—sometimes we would laugh about how nothing seemed to flow. But with a daily commentary also came strict deadlines. Well, they were supposed to be strict. Don't tell anyone, but I did a fair amount of rewriting in the studio (I like them fresh). When we first started in June 1998, just before we moved to the television studio, our producer, John Sorensen, would conclude some of our sessions with the words, "Well, that was about as easy as pulling teeth." Other times, after I asked him how a particular commentary sounded, he would use the words, "Only perfect." I think that was to prevent any further rewrites.

I sometimes had to remind myself to enjoy the process. Of course, that's something we all should be doing as a rule anyway, don't you think? Usually that was the case, but sometimes it takes more effort than others.

And I'm told I wasn't always the gentlest of editors. When I interviewed Bob Carter as the CENTER's director of communications, I asked him to write a commentary for the interview. After reading it, I commented that he took "a good stab at it." This quote tended to come up from time to time. But it was great that he wasn't bitter about it.

We would discover something new about Bob in virtually every commentary session—in fact, it became a joke—the guy was into everything. Brandon Aronson was reading a made-up commentary one day about how the "C" in SCUBA stood for "Carter." Bob responded, "I missed that one on my lifeguard test." We all just looked at each other—yes, Bob was a lifeguard, in addition to being a pastor, lawyer, piano player, roller skater, singer, and our first commentary writer.

Greg Hoadley, the intern-turned head writer was the MVP of the commentaries. Greg is the absolute best researcher I have ever met. He finds stuff no one else can. But I guess that happens when you read everything that's out there. He now writes news articles for the CENTER's website, www.reclaimamerica.org.

He and Bob reminisced that some of the commentaries into which they poured their heart and soul wouldn't even get the privilege of being read aloud. They would get the, "Ah-no" from me. Brutal. Every once in a while however, there would be a perfect, un-editable commentary that got the stars, smiley faces and 100 percent notations, and would decorate the walls of each of the crew: Greg Hoadley, Bob Carter, Brandon Aronson, Jim Carter, Rich DeFilippo, and Chris Gorbey. A phenomenal group of guys.

Chris, who now directs the Communication Department of the CENTER, insisted that I include some of what went into these little gems. For some reason he thought people would want to know how you take a group of people that seem normal enough and end up with commentaries like these. How does one take stacks of research and "Janetize" it for broadcast?

When Bob became a full-time pastor in July 1999, we were fortunate to land his brother Jim as a replacement. I asked Jim to write some commentaries for the interview which aired before he was even hired! How's *that* for good stewardship?

Then there's Rich DeFilippo: crime-fighting commentary writer by day, web designer by night.

Here's one of Rich's that aired "unedited":

> The folks at the World Wrestling Federation are at it again. This time they're suing because their show, WWF Smackdown, criticized as being "the most ultra-violent, foul-mouthed, and sexually explicit show on prime time" is losing sponsors. The Parent's Television Council has exposed the truth about this program and sponsors are withdrawing their support. This has made the folks at the WWF mad! They've tried everything from threatening letters, to mocking the PTC's president regularly on the show. Those efforts have failed so now they're suing, claiming that they have been "Injured" by the PTC's efforts to dissuade advertisers from sponsoring the show. Looks like "the Bad Boys of Television" aren't so tough after all!

I found it hanging on his wall with a star, smiley face, "100 percent" "Wow!" and "You Rock!" He's now working on the web full time. Click on www.reclaimamerica.org and you'll see why.

Thanks too, to Stacey Mossop (who did my make-up) and Angela Guerrera, who told me which clothes "all the cool kids were wearing."

I really enjoyed the two-and-a-half years we did the commentaries, and am very appreciative to Vic Eliason, whose idea to also do the commentaries in a television version, led to the leap of faith that eventually took these commentaries to 200 television stations, along with the 300 radio stations that aired them daily.

Vic's little idea also moved us from the radio studio to the television studio, where we worked with some very cool people like John Quarquesso (whom we all affectionately refer to as "Q"), who directed most of our television commentaries. On one particularly rough day, Q brought candy to throw at me. It was a pretty nice gesture, really- breaking up the seriousness and focus of not getting it perfect and making it fun again. I always *thought* of it as a "nice gesture" but, come to think about it, maybe he just liked to throw things at me. In any event, it livened things up. Rebecca Roberts, a former intern with the CENTER, sometimes filled in as TV director. I'm not sure she had the proper training, however. Instead of "action" she would say, "GO!" or "SPEAK!"

Barry Kase, our Media Relations guru, helped in the television expansion, set, and came up with brilliant ideas like—maybe you should have someone do your make-up for these things!

My crew was not above practical jokes, either. You

see, once I heard that word "action," I would automatically start reading from the teleprompter, and on one particular occasion they had a slightly edited version for me to read (read the next paragraph out loud, and you'll see what I mean):

Just last month the Supreme Court heard arguments on partial-birth abortion. The usual pro-abortion groups were there, as always. But so was a group of passionate, pro-life pastors, who peacefully protested, pontificating their pro-life proclamation on printed pamphlets, which were passed out on the paved public parkway.

Needless to say, they had fun watching me trying to get through all the "p's." As you would expect, I never got past the fifth line.

So why is it *30 Seconds to Common Sense* and not sixty? Well, with the introduction and ending, there was only 37 seconds of actual commentary. That's if you read them aloud. Now, while I talk pretty fast, I'm still pretty sure you can read them silently even faster. Perhaps even *faster* than 30 seconds.

While on the road speaking, I had an opportunity to talk to many of the people who listened to the *Reclaiming America with Janet Folger* commentaries. Some said they sat in their cars before going into work just to hear them. Others said it gave them the ammunition they needed for their liberal college professors. But my favorite was a woman from Michigan who told me she was my "biggest fan," and then introduced me to a senator who she had listen "every single day from 2-4:00." They were listening to Janet *Parshall*.

The same thing happened at the National Religious Broadcaster's meeting when one woman asked me if I had been on 20/20 the night before. When I told her that I had, I was feeling pretty good about myself. It's kind of cool having someone recognize you. That was until she rushed up and gave me a great big hug, saying, "I love you Janet *Parshall*." I love her, too.

The coolest thing was when I was on Janet Parshall's show and she told me she had someone tell her "they love what she's doing with RECLAIMING AMERICA." At least she didn't recognize my voice! (*just kidding!*)

Many thanks to everyone who listened and watched the *Reclaiming America with Janet Folger* commentaries in the past two-and-a-half years, and thanks too, to all of you who read them. And while this brief look at the inside jokes and stories behind them doesn't do justice to the good times we had putting them together, I hope it shows you that just because you're "fighting the forces of evil" doesn't mean you can't have fun doing it.

The early TV team: Courtney Urbanek, me, Lisa Velazquez and John Q at the Christmas party.

Here we are playing reindeer games after taping one day in December. (From left to right: Chris Gorbey, Soraya Rodriquez-Fisher, Barry Kase, Barbara Collier, Carol Krpata, Greg Hoadley, Maxine Makas, Rich DeFilippo. [Bottom] Angela Guerrera and me.)